Breaking the Cage

A Woman's Memoir of Freedom, Dreams, Defiance, and Breaking Traditions

Nasso Haymour

AUTHORITY
PUBLISHING

ISBN (Paperback): 978-1-965480-16-8

ISBN (eBook): 978-1-965480-14-4

Published by: Authority Publishing

www.authority-publishing.com

Printed in the United States of America.

This is for the one who never let me lose myself in this scary world—my angel in heaven, my dad.

To my great-grandmother Zhur Haymour, who passed away, but her soul guided me to the right path.

To Maria Isabel Tostes Bueno, who believed in me, inspired me, and treated me like her daughter all these years.

To all the women in my family who screamed so loud and yet were never heard.

Contents

"Don't Push The River, It Flows By itself." — Barry Stevens

Message From The Author

This book is for you—the dreamer for the person who wakes up every day fighting to make a dream come true. I know how hard it can be. Sometimes, we feel demotivated and unsupported by the people around us: friends, partners, and even our families. Sometimes, it feels like every door is closed, like things are moving too slowly, or like we're stuck in place, but if there's one thing I've learned over the years, it's this:

"Patience is everything."

What is meant for you will always find its way to you. It doesn't matter if there's an ocean in the middle or mountains blocking your path; sooner or later, it will be yours. It's okay to take a break when you feel tired. It's okay to pause, to catch your breath, but what's not okay is giving up halfway down the road. If there's something stuck in your mind, something your soul craves so deeply that it keeps you awake at night, then it's worth chasing. It's worth every sacrifice to make it a reality.

"Dreams" isn't just a word for children, despite what some people may say. Dreams are what give us hope. They save us from the cruel realities of this world. Don't wait for support or recognition to push you forward. Don't waste time trying to please society. The motivation and dedication have to come from you.

Another thing life has taught me is this: do things in silence. The envy of others sleeps lightly, and the evil eye can wake easily. Don't shout your plans from the rooftops. Protect your dreams as you work on them. Do the hard work in silence, for you, and only for you, never to impress others.

Dreams come true like mine did, but the road there might take you through hell. You might get burned, and the scars you carry will tell the story of your triumphs. Those scars will be the stories you'll share one day with your children, grandchildren, nieces and nephews, or even just with your pets. They are proof of your resilience, your strength, and your belief in yourself.

Never let anyone decide your future for you. You are the author of your own story. People will try to bring you down. They'll tell you "you're not good enough," that the job you want is too competitive," that the "odds are too slim." They'll say, "It's not for you. Maybe try something else." But remember this: someone has to be chosen. So why not you? Just because something didn't work out for someone else doesn't mean it won't work out for you. There are billions of stars in the sky, and every single one of them shines differently. That's how it works for us, too. Each of us shines in our unique way.

So don't let anyone dim your light. Don't give up on your dreams because someone else says they're too difficult to achieve. You can be anything you want to be as long as you believe in yourself, timing, and destiny.

Be kind to yourself. Trust the journey. Everything is already written; everything is written (Maktoub).

مكتوب

CHAPTER I

Not Marriage Material

مش ست بيت

"Hi, Nesrin! I just wanted to take this opportunity to say it was nice knowing you during our time together.

I know that my son, your husband—soon to be ex-husband—because he finally called it quits, and he's standing firm regarding his decision.

Why did you marry him if you never wanted to be part of his life as a wife? Why make him lose four years of his life with you if you always knew you would never quit your job to be his life partner, best friend, and, more importantly, love? Was he just a checkmark on your bucket list? You had every opportunity to quit your job, be with him, and assume your role as a wife.

This is a marriage, not a pinball game, for you bounce the ball in any direction. You have all the papers in your hand to come to Canada, but instead, you want to keep your waitress-in-the-sky job and travel around the world.

He's a man full of responsibilities in life. Who will pay his mortgages? His rent? Of course, it won't be you because he makes triple what you make.

Was my son just a status for you? I want you to look around and see that all your family and friends are either about to get married, got married, or are starting a family, and those who aren't eventually will be soon.

You know what's going to happen to you? You will be left all alone with your cats. Do you not have any remorse or empathy for everything you've been doing? He gave you everything; he supported your career as a flight attendant.

What other man would have done that or accepted his wife traveling around and sleeping in hotels? Men like Samir are rare. Samir has moved on, Al Hamdulilah.

In Islam, he has the right as a man to remarry at any time because in Islam, you are not, and did not, fulfill your wifely duties, and he has the right to move on and find his future wife, life partner, best friend, and love.

He has already found someone to help him build his empire. Behind every great man, a greater woman stood by him and his dreams, and you are not that woman. I'm telling you Samir is already with another wife; she knows about you and has accepted it.

She will live in their brand-new condo or house, whatever she chooses, and he will give her all the support she needs to do whatever she wants in life. So, Nesrin, it's time for him to move on without you.

Your book is finished, and it's time for him to write a new one with a new beginning with someone else."

I was at The Dubai Mall with my two friends, Rami and Glenda, when I received this message from my mother-in-law saying that my husband was married to someone else, simply because I wouldn't give up on my flight attendant career to live in Canada with Samir and be his unpaid maid.

I read the message out loud to my friends with a trembling voice. It felt like I had a rock stuck in my throat while reading it.

The tears started to fall, then I put the phone down, covered my face with my two hands, and started to cry like a kid who had lost her favorite blanket. Glenda hugged me and said:

"Don't let any of those hurtful words affect you. You shouldn't be held responsible for him choosing to marry someone else. He would have made this decision if you were a flight attendant or a stay-at-home wife."

Rami joined the hug and said, "It's Samir's loss. Everything your mother-in-law said reflects her twisted vision of you and not the real you. Don't let her get into your head."

They held my hand and said I deserved someone who would respect me and my career.

They reminded me that it's better to end up alone with five cats in the house watching Netflix while eating pizza than to be stuck with a man who believes a wife was made to clean, cook, and deliver as many kids as he desires.

They made me feel better, calmed me down, and made me take deep breaths and think clearly.

I knew I had to put myself back together, leave that gigantic mall, head home, call my dad, who lived in São Paulo, and tell him that he had been right this entire time. Baba was always against me getting married to Samir, and he was never a fan of him.

I guess he always felt that Samir wasn't the one for me.

I met Samir through my high school friend, who happened to be his cousin. His cousin knew I was single and thought we'd be a good match.

Samir ticked all the boxes for me: tall, muscular, with green eyes, brown hair, and the perfect beard. Best of all, he was Canadian with a Lebanese background.

He spoke flawless Arabic and seemed like the romantic, family-oriented man I'd always dreamed of. That's how it all started.

Samir lived in Canada while I was based in Dubai. We made it work. I operated flights to Toronto every month and spent my layovers with him. We traveled together, adopted a dog, cooked meals in his cozy apartment, and explored Canada.

It felt perfect—like a fairy tale. We rarely fought, and I was convinced nothing could come between us. But then came the million-dollar question: "When will you resign from your job?"

Honestly, I had seen it coming. Every time I got to know an Arab man, they would ask when I was resigning from my job because, in society's mind, a flight attendant cannot get married and have a family.

My answer was always the same, and it was the answer I gave to Samir: "Whoever wants to be with me must accept my career."

Of course, they would never accept my answer because they only wanted a housewife, not an independent wife they could not control. Samir was no different.

He wanted me to give it all up for him, live in Canada by his side, and be the wife he envisioned—a housewife who cooked, cleaned, and waited for him at the door, not a wife he would wonder about in terms of which country or hotel she was sleeping in.

I told him, "If you can't accept my chosen career and path, then we are not meant to be together."

I was devastated because I liked him. I thought that because he was born and raised in Canada, he would have a different mentality than the other guys—a less rigid mindset, an open mind, and a more Westernized way of living—but he didn't.

We went a couple of weeks without talking. I wanted to message him and tell him how much I wanted to be with him multiple times, but sending him a text meant giving up on everything I had fought hard to achieve.

I had been through hell and back, lied, cheated, hurt people, humiliated myself, and cried my eyes out day after day, all to gain my independence and fly the world.

And I couldn't accept throwing it all away because someone didn't accept my chosen path or career.

I wondered if it would have been different if he were a male flight attendant or pilot. That wouldn't have been a problem, but it was unacceptable because I was a woman traveling.

A few weeks passed, and he texted me, saying we should be together no matter what. He never stopped thinking about me and said that we were a perfect match, that we had chemistry, and that he would accept and understand my routine and career.

I didn't know where things were going from there, but my heart jumped with happiness. After one year of dating, he proposed to me with an improvised promise ring.

We made plans for our future, dreamed together, and made important decisions: he would move to Dubai, and we would start a new life together.

When I told Baba about the engagement, he wasn't thrilled. On the phone, he said, with a very angry voice, "What do you want with marriage now? You don't need that. You are working, traveling, and living your dreams. Marriage can wait."

At first, he refused to meet Samir, upset and protective as any father would be, but after my mom calmed him down, he relented: "Do whatever makes you happy; do whatever makes you comfortable.

If there's one thing I have learned, it's to stop telling you what not to do because you will still go and do it behind my back."

I guess he was a bit jealous as well. I have two brothers: Walid, the oldest, and Hamza, the youngest.

But I was always Daddy's princess—the middle child, the only girl, the spoiled one—and seeing his daughter growing up, wanting to get married, and having another man take care of her activated his anger and jealousy like any other father would feel.

He wasn't happy and tried to change my mind about marriage multiple times, saying, "When we wanted you to get married, you didn't want to.

Now you change your mind?" "Don't you feel too young? Twenty-five years old is young for marriage." "You are living your dream; you don't need this responsibility now."

But as usual, I never listened to anyone and always went against any opinion given to me. I was in love, and I wanted a partner. I was tired of arriving home with nobody waiting for me, cooking, eating, and living alone.

The life of a flight attendant is wonderful, glamorous, and adventurous. I discovered new cultures and religions, attended midnight parties, and made friends all over the world, but it can also get very lonely.

Also, I think I was feeling pressured by the people around me and society. Everybody around me was getting married—my cousins, my friends. They were happy, and I wanted that happiness as well.

After two years of dating, we got married in our village in Lebanon. Our wedding was like a fairy tale. He came to pick me up on a horse, along with a "Zaffe" and his family, and they were all riding horses.

They performed a traditional Arabic dance under my house before picking me up. Our wedding was called the vintage wedding, with vintage chairs, real blue and pink flowers everywhere, and wooden tables and chairs that looked rustic.

A small brown bag of scented flowers that I got from Shanghai, China, with the message "Thank you for witnessing our always and forever," was placed on top of each plate for the guests as our wedding souvenir.

The celebration took place in an open space with a view of our village's lake, with 800 people dancing and celebrating our love.

Little did I know that "always and forever" were just empty words printed on paper that would later end up in the bin. I thought marriage was like a fairy tale, and everything would be beautiful and filled with sunny days, just like my wedding day.

Unfortunately, my marriage was most of the time like an airplane passing through turbulence, and I kept my seat belt buckled and tight, scared of hitting the airplane ceiling and dying.

I got home from the mall with my head exploding. I needed a break, so I switched off my phone. I needed to put myself back together and process everything that was going on. I knew my marriage wasn't perfect and wasn't working well.

I knew at some point we would get divorced, but divorce is never easy. A house being broken is never easy. I was in pain, I was hurt, and I was afraid of being alone again. I took a sleeping pill and only woke up after eight hours.

When I switched on my phone, I found thousands of messages on WhatsApp, missed calls from my Baba, missed calls from my cousins in Lebanon, and many screenshots. I opened one of my cousin Rayan's chats.

She had screenshots of Samir's Instagram post, stating that we were divorced. He wrote the date of our marriage and the date of our divorce, making everything public.

My heart dropped. The entire village where I was from in Lebanon had seen his posts. Rayan confirmed it: "People are already calling our families to get all the gossip. The phone doesn't stop ringing."

I couldn't believe what was happening. I never cared about people talking behind my back, about reputation, or any of that. Samir made our divorce public without even talking to me, and what hurt me the most was the disrespect.

I panicked; I was sure the news had already reached my parents' ears.

I called my Baba straight away, and as soon as he picked up the call, he started shouting angrily, "Who does he think he is to talk about my daughter like that? Does he think he can destroy my daughter's reputation? I swear he will regret it."

Through tears, I explained everything to Baba. I was caught off guard by the news of the divorce and the Instagram post he had spread around, shaming our marriage.

"Announcing what?" Baba demanded, furious and wanting to know what was going on.

"What did he announce? What did he post? I don't have Instagram. I don't know anything.

Your father-in-law just called me on Samir's behalf, saying you are getting divorced because you haven't fulfilled your duties as a wife and are not marriage material. But don't worry; I put him in his place.

He will have to think twice before ever calling me to discuss my daughter again."

I was crying on the phone, apologizing to Baba for not listening to him and for rushing to get married. I told him I was lost and didn't know what to do. My phone was full of messages.

People in the village were pressuring me, and Baba said to me in a soft and supportive voice, "Don't be lost. Pack your things, go to Lebanon, and divorce the rubbish."

Baba's words hit me like a lifeline. His unwavering support gave me the strength I needed to face everything. He said with a steady voice, full of pride and love:

"You are my daughter. No one can define your worth—not him, his family, or anyone. You are stronger than this. You have already survived more than they will ever know. Now, it's time to take back your life."

I sat on the cold floor of my living room, with my cats all around me and my phone in hand, letting his words sink in. For so long, I had been afraid of disappointing Baba and proving his warnings wrong.

But then, I realized it wasn't about proving anyone right or wrong. It was about reclaiming my dignity, my strength, and my independence. After we hung up, I sat there for a while, staring out the window, trying to make sense of everything.

The humiliation of Samir's Instagram post, the gossip spreading through the village, and my mother-in-law's venomous words all felt heavy and suffocating.

But then I thought about the life I had built for myself, the dreams I had fought so hard for, and I knew I couldn't let this break me.

Chapter 2

You Can Go to Paris, and He Can Go to Hell

انتي روحي باريس وهو الى الجحيم

I landed in Lebanon and knew that the war was starting. I faced two significant challenges: overcoming my divorce and navigating society. My uncle Mosab and Aunt Rufaida were waiting for me at Rafik Hariri airport. He always had a smile on his face, and she was ready with the warmest hugs.

Aunt Rufaida was the one who always looked after me through the years, considering me as her oldest daughter, and Mosab was the one who always gave me career path advice and always made jokes I never understood, and yet he would make me laugh somehow. When I visited Lebanon, I would always stay at their house since I felt safe and loved there.

They have two daughters, Ikram and Youmna, who consider me an older sister. They are proud of who I have become and consider me an example to them.

They would always say that I was the one who broke traditions, stereotypes, and strict rules to become independent and free, someone all the girls in that village aspired to be. But at the airport, I was so broken that I felt like a complete failure. I felt like I had let down all the girls who looked up to me for inspiration. I had let people step on me until I was out of breath.

Aunt Rufaida hugged me unconditionally at the airport. At the same time, I cried, telling me that she would never let anything happen to me, that I was strong, and that everything, even the worst storms, was temporary. She asked me not to be ashamed of my divorce and that some things must end for other beautiful things to happen in our lives.

"And perhaps you hate something, and it is better for you, and perhaps you love something, and it is evil for you, and God knows, and you do not know," she said in Arabic, bringing peace to my heart.

"ٍء عسى ان تكرهوا شيناً وهو خيرٌ لكم
وعسى ان تحبوا شيناً وهو شرٌ لكم والله
يعلم وانتم لا تعلمون"

She quoted a strong phrase from the Holy Koran, and she meant that bad things usually happen to us for our own good. Sometimes, we want something so badly to work out, but it will only harm us, and God's plan is stronger than any plan we make in life. Her words felt like flowers blooming inside me, bringing peace to my soul and calming me down.

That's all I needed: support from my family during that difficult time. I felt someone holding my hand while I was passing through a street without any illumination, scared of an abomination.

It's a 2-hour drive from the airport to the countryside of Lebanon, where I am from. It's a long drive, but I always enjoy it. I admire the view, the mountains, the wineries, and the houses resembling castles. I always keep the car window down so I can smell the fresh air. I have always loved Lebanon and everything that it has to offer.

Even with their political mess and the economic crisis, it's a beautiful country to live in. The only thing is that I always felt like I didn't belong there. I have an open mind, a different mentality, and a different point of view; feminism was ingrained in me from birth. I support women's rights, and the fact that women don't get the recognition they deserve frustrates me.

Lebanon is a wonderful country that I love, but it has rules and traditions that I hate. I arrived at their house, and my entire family was there, all my uncles, aunts, and cousins. I got the hugs, motivation, and support to go through this divorce. The phone wouldn't stop ringing, and the entire village wanted to know what was happening with my marriage and me.

At some point, my family just stopped answering the phone. Mosab said, "Everybody is chewing you, but don't worry, this shall stop once they find another bubble gum to chew."

I was different; I was the first female flight attendant from that part of Lebanon ever hired. Nobody ever ventured against their families as I did. Their constant worry was, "What will people say?" "What should happen if no man marries me?" Parents hardly let their girls study alone in Beirut, the capital, two hours from our village.

Imagine allowing them to traverse the globe and live elsewhere. Still, I did it; I did all they instructed a woman not to do, which set me apart. Everyone knew who I was in my village and throughout the countryside.

Often seen in the streets, people would ask me if I was a "flight attendant." Curious about my personal life, my schedule, which places I have visited, and whether I would be afraid of a plane disaster or if I get tired of flying life. I had to answer many questions everywhere I went and at every residence I entered.

I remember one day I was operating a Dubai—Beirut flight, and one of the passengers heard me speaking Arabic and asked me which part of Lebanon I was in; once I told him, another passenger jumped and said with a smiley face and confidence, "You are Khaled Haymour's daughter, aren't you?"

I nodded and said "yes" with a firm voice, proud of who I was and where I had come from. That man knew exactly who I was and my story; he wasn't even someone from my village. I guess every village in the world is the same. Everybody knows everybody. Everybody wants to interfere in everyone's life. The rumors and gossiping don't matter, regardless of which culture or religion they follow; they're all the same.

"I have booked an appointment for tomorrow with the Sheikh who performed your marriage to discuss the divorce and your rights," said my uncle Mosab while we were all gathered at the table having lunch.

When I finally forgot my life tragedies for a few minutes and enjoyed lunch with the people I loved the most, my cousin Rayan got a notification on her phone and screamed, "It's a message from Samir."

Saying he had changed his mind, he texted her, forwarding a message to me. He wants the divorce no longer. In Islam, he is permitted to marry three more; hence, he will remain wed to me. He knew he would have to pay me all my rights as a Muslim woman should he seek a divorce, and he was too stingy to do that. Should I seek a divorce, he would give me absolutely nothing.

Samir also mentioned he would move forward and marry whoever he wanted while still married to me. He would make sure I hung around suffering and was unable to move on with my life. For everything I had done to him, he wanted me to pay. My decision to choose my flight attendant job over him was unacceptable and disrespectful from his perspective.

I made him feel small in front of his parents and society. I was supposed to obey his requests as a married woman. But Samir didn't understand that he met me in uniform, knew about my career and job, and always knew that I would never leave my career for any man or family member. I never forced him to do anything.

No one had a loaded gun in his forehead and forced him to build a life with a flight attendant. He accepted me the way I was. He moved to Dubai of his own free will. And I wasn't going to change a thing for him or anybody. It was court day; I woke up early to prepare the clothes I was supposed to wear.

I picked a long-sleeved black shirt reaching my thighs that, in another world, girls would wear as a dress. Blue jeans and sandals. I was going to a Muslim court, so I dressed accordingly. You cannot enter the court wearing anything short or showing too much skin. It's considered disrespectful, especially while going to meet a sheik. My uncle Mosab and I were on our way to court.

It was two villages away from ours, approximately a 10-minute drive. We got a call from the Sheikh saying there was a change of plans; he had to rush home and asked if we could meet him at his place. We agreed and continued to his house, only two minutes from the court.

When we arrived there, I had everything printed: the chats, the messages I got from his family, my mother-in-law's letter, and everything that I needed to start the divorce process, but the Sheikh barely looked at them. Instead, he asked, "Aren't you a flight attendant?"

In a soft, low voice, I nodded and said, "Yes, I work for Dubai Airways."

He made a sarcastic smile and shook his head from side to side. Keeping a sarcastic face, he commented, "Yeah, I don't blame him for wanting to remarry. I don't like this kind of job; they are not for family girls."

I looked at him with a face of disbelief. His words felt like someone had just punched me in my stomach and left me on the floor with internal bleeding, and yet, I didn't let him finish me; I said, "He met me while I wore that uniform; it's a job like any other. He decided to build a life with someone else, and I can't control that."

"Yes. What makes you believe that's the case? Because he needs a wife by his side and not a flight attendant," said the Sheikh, answering as if he was carrying a bunch of sticks and stones and throwing them at me.

I was speechless because of the way I was treated there. Everything was my fault. He meant that I destroyed my marriage because I am a flight attendant. Because I have a job that requires traveling? I didn't get any support from Sheikh. My mind was filled with a plethora of thoughts; however, I was unable to articulate them. The words simply would not emerge; he was able to subdue me with his words.

I felt intimidated by him, and everything I would say wouldn't matter because, in his mind, I was wrong for choosing a career that wasn't appropriate for a Muslim married woman. So, I kept quiet and swallowed all my words. Uncle Mosab didn't say a word as well. We didn't want any confrontation at a Sheikh's house.

He said he was going to send the divorce papers to Canada, but he could not force Samir to sign them, and if he wanted to marry someone else while married to me, it was his legal right as a Muslim man.

Uncle Mosab politely thanked him for his assistance, while in my mind, I was picturing myself throwing him down the stairs for not supporting me as a young, independent woman and blaming me for destroying an already broken marriage.

On our way out of his house, the sheik shouted my name and said, "Nesrin, please, next time you come to my house, wear an abaya and a hijab." I entered the car, and immediately, I started to cry. Mosab told me to calm down and not to let the Sheikh's words affect me, but it was too late; I already had psychological damage. I couldn't understand why they saw me this way.

Instead of being proud of me for being the first flight attendant from the region to reach an international airline and make a name for myself, they should be happy that I am working, supporting my family, and being independent. I'm not depending on anyone or any man.

"I just don't think it's fair that the guy who does money laundering and drugs comes and builds a castle in the village, marries the prettiest girls, and still gets all the respect from everybody in town, even from the Sheikh and me, who is working hard, saving money to build a future for myself, and I get disrespected? And seeing as a whore in the skies? Is this how people see me here? As a rule breaker? A rebel? Or someone with a lost soul?"

With my chest heavy and with a rapid breath I could not control, I said those things to my uncle in a frustrated voice. Mosab replied that while people in that village viewed me differently, what I said was untrue. They would prefer to see me married, living in a house with a husband and children, aging with them, and not flying from nation to nation.

They were raised and think this way; there is nothing we can do to alter their perspective. Mosab advised me to keep my head clear of all the negativity and gossiping hurled at me. He advised us to head to a grocery store, choose some snacks, and have Aunt Rufaida and the daughters have a family movie night. It would ease my discomfort.

I agreed, and we went to the neighborhood grocery near the house so I could pick the Takis chips that Youmna and Ikram liked the most.

Everyone turned to see me as soon as I walked into the grocery. The whispers let me notice some girls chatting with one another and staring at me. Uncomfortable, I hurried to the aisle with all the chocolates and snacks to quickly get all I needed for our movie night and leave there. I noticed two older women gossiping in the other aisle as I gathered the fiery Takis my cousins adore.

They sounded as if they wanted me to hear their chat and were loud. Sure, they are divorcing naturally? Who would desire a woman who jumps from plane to plane? Blood was boiling inside my body. I aspired to slam Takis chips into their faces, and this time, I would not be ashamed to remain silent; an overwhelming rage began to develop within me.

With my cheeks and ears scarlet, ready to start a scene, I was coming towards them when Mosab came up to take me by the arm, dropped the snacks I had in hand, and sent me directly from the supermarket to the car. I asked him to let go of me because I wanted to put these women in their place, but he said firmly, "Not here. Not here, not while you are with me. I am a well-respected teacher in this village, and I will not allow you to put yourself or me through shame and give this person what they want: more reason to chew you and eat you alive. You can smash her face a thousand times or stab her in your mind thousands of times. It will not change anything. You would complicate more things, and they will never leave you alone."

He was right; this was what they wanted. They would relish the opportunity to witness me losing my composure and disseminating additional gossip about Samir's justified decision to move on with another woman. I had to be the bigger person here and learn to control my emotions to win this fight. We arrived home. I hugged my cousins Youmna and Ikram, who I consider sisters; despite an 18- and 15-year gap between us, we were always very close.

Even with my crazy career, busy schedule, and flying life, I still saw them growing up. I was always present and by their side in the bad and the good moments. They have been there for me, too, when I needed them. Youmna is 18 years old and getting ready to go to university. Making her dream of becoming a psychologist come true.

Ikram is in her last year of high school and is a little indecisive about what she wants to become, but she will figure it out. She's a smart girl. Believe it or not, they are the ones who keep giving me life advice and motivational speeches when I feel down and about to give up on everything.

We had no movie night; I arrived empty-handed, and we never did anything without snacks. I was too ashamed of leaving the house and too scared to show my face to the world and let them witness my misery. It was 1:00 AM bedtime, but Ikram always wanted to talk before we slept. She would ask many questions about life outside that village; sometimes, I never had the right answer for her.

It's a big world full of mysteries and unanswered questions, and I still have a lot to discover, but I always try to share my experiences with my failures and triumphs. I'm always trying to prepare them for a world they haven't seen yet. As always curious about my flight attendant life, Ikram asked, "Are there any flight attendants who wear hijab?"

I smiled softly because I felt she wanted to become one someday and travel the world like I did. However, she was scared that the hijab on her head would be a reason for rejection. I reassured her that her cultural beliefs and religion would not hinder her from realizing her dream. "Of course there is. You can work for a Saudi or Malaysian airline.

They have a special uniform for ladies in hijab."

When I thought we were finally going to sleep, Youmna asked another question: "Is it true that my dad helped you become a flight attendant? I overheard him speaking to my mom about this subject."

"Yes, Youmna, your parents supported me when everybody was against me. This was years ago. You were young. Maybe that's why you don't remember. I had these dreams; I needed to chase them, but on my way chasing them, I fell. People started to step on me, and they were among the few who extended their hands and helped me get up."

She jumped on the bed where Ikram and I were sleeping and softly said, "I am sorry for everything happening to you. You don't deserve it. And I want you to know that I am proud of you and the person you have become. To us and many girls in this village, you are an inspiration. Many girls in my school know you and have always wanted to meet you."

Tears were falling down my face from the kind words. They were real, and they touched my soul. The three of us hugged. Ikram started to dry the tears coming down my face and said, "Don't worry about Samir and all the nasty things. Girl, you are a flight attendant! You can go to Paris, and he can go to hell." I laughed so hard at her comment.

It was cute and, at the same time, powerful, and she was right. I'm a flight attendant. I can go anywhere I want, and then I promised them I would go to Paris when all this is over to recharge my energies, eat some macaroons while staring at the Eiffel Tower, and forget all this mess. "I'm not sleepy, I'm not going to sleep, and you're not allowed to sleep."

Can you please tell us everything that happened? How did you become a flight attendant? How did it start?"

Ikram said excitedly, and Youmna made herself comfortable in the bed, waiting to hear the story. They were both wide awake, refusing to sleep. I wasn't sleepy either. Then I agreed to tell them everything, but I warned them that for them to understand how it all started, I must go back to when I was 12 years old; their attention was all on me.

CHAPTER 3

Wild Rose

الورد البري

Baba was a very hard-working man. He never had much luck with money or work, but he always tried his best to provide us with everything we needed. He kept moving from country to country, chasing jobs, and he would always take us with him.

He lived in Brazil, where my siblings and I were born, but things didn't work out very well for him, so Baba moved to Colombia and took us with him. Colombia was the place where I had the best childhood memories.

The place where I made friends, learned how to write and read, developed a personality, and met the most kindhearted people. There was a huge community of Lebanese in Colombia working there. Work was fire, and I remembered that my dad had a store; he used to sell fans, and things were going well.

We had a huge, nicely furnished apartment. I had my bedroom, with air conditioning, a computer, many Barbies, and nice girly clothes. His work was finally going well, and he provided us with everything a family needs.

As we know, nothing lasts forever. Life is like a roller coaster: "One day you are up, and then suddenly you are down." That's part of life. Colombia had a significant economic crisis in 2002.

All the Arabs there started to leave the country, searching for other possibilities and taking their families with them. Stores were getting closed, and my dad's store was one of them. The costs started to mount up; Baba determined that we should leave Colombia forever.

He told my mom that he would travel back to Brazil and try his luck there one more time, but he would go alone.

My mother decided she should return to Lebanon to be near her parents. Moving from country to country fatigued her. My parents then decided that moving to Lebanon would be the greatest choice for us four. Baba wanted his children to learn Arabic, the religion, and the culture.

Growing up in a country far from all that worried my parents constantly. They worried we would lose the connection we have with the Arab world. I vividly recall my brothers and I crying to say goodbye to Baba.

It would be the first time we had been split apart, and we had no idea when we would be together again as a family. He promised we would meet each other soon; I assured him I would write him letters. On our journey to Lebanon, we flew Middle Eastern Airlines.

My brothers and I were debating who would have the window seat. Walid won since he was the oldest child. Hamza had the middle seat. I took the aisle seat, and my mom was seated on the other side of the aisle next to me.

One Lebanese flight attendant was quite fluent in Spanish. She began to chat with us. She wanted to know whether our move to Lebanon excited us. She had blue eyes, blonde hair, and an earring shaped like a pearl, and she was gorgeous. She was so sophisticated; I could smell her floral scent. Wearing that flight attendant attire, she exuded great importance.

Her natural attractiveness captivated me. At the time, I believed she was the most beautiful woman I had ever seen. She gave me an orange juice, and when she handed it to me, I looked her in the eyes and told her, "I want to be like you when I grow up." She smiled with her perfectly aligned white teeth and told me I could be anything I wanted once I turned 18.

We arrived at Beirut airport, and the entire family was waiting for us. I remember Aunt Rufaida running to hug me and my other cousins. I didn't know anyone then; it was my first time meeting the family. Then I saw my cousin, Rayan.

She hugged me, and we walked towards the car, hugging as if we had known each other for years.

We didn't have a place of our own yet, so we stayed at my grandparents' house for months. My dad was broke; he didn't have money to send us to rent a place. He would always call and say that things in Brazil were hard, and he barely made any money to survive.

I remember my mom taking us to another village to sell her gold without anyone seeing it, away from people's eyes. She didn't want people to see how much we were struggling financially.

She sold a piece of gold monthly to pay our school fees and expenses until nothing was left, only her wedding band on her finger. We didn't have money for anything not to buy for our personal needs.

I remember when it was Eid day, the holy celebration for Muslims, and the tradition was that everybody wore new clothes. Still, my mom didn't have money to buy us new clothes, so I used to wear Rayan's old clothes, which she had worn only once on previous Eids.

This was our life—entirely different from what it was in Colombia. We lived in our grandparents' house, receiving financial help from family members, accepting clothes and shoe donations, book donations for school, and even the uniform.

We wouldn't go out much because there were days when my mom didn't even have money to buy us an ice cream. It was a daily struggle for her; she had to raise three kids alone and depend on people's donations to survive.

My siblings and I were too young to understand her suffering, and we only woke up to the reality of our past when we grew up.

My mother drove me to see her grandma, whose name matched hers, "Zhur," one morning. She was eighty years old and lived alone in a somewhat small room. Years ago, my great-grandmother was living in Brazil and would have assisted my mother however she could have.

She was like a mother to her, more than a grandma; she was present every time my mom was at the hospital delivering. She showed her how to treat a newborn and never left her side. Seeing her grandma live in a shoebox infuriated Mama; the room just had a bed and a TV—nothing else.

Her youngest daughter, Aunt Fatima, who had recently relocated to Lebanon, would shower and cook her food; my grandfather would always take her to spend the day in his house. And nobody would ask, visit, or send money for the other of her sons.

None wanted to be in charge of looking after an elderly lady. She was crying as she told my mother about how some of her children and sons were treating her and that she hadn't even communicated with a few of them in years.

My mom was narrating stories to me about my great-grandma, how she was a strong woman in the past, used to work hard, raised nine children, had seven miscarriages, and for what when we left her house? To be left alone in a shoebox is when my mother got a great idea and said, "What if I recommend that my uncles open a house for us? They pay the rent while we look after Grandma Zhur."

The same way Grandma Zhur looked after me so wonderfully in Brazil when I had nobody.

I told her that would be a smart move. We would care for her; she was too old to be by herself. Auntie Fatima would continue to help us with everything, and we would finally have a place to call our own. We would help them, and they would help us. And everyone would be happy.

Later that day, my mom reunited all her uncles and aunts and proposed to them. We helped them, and they helped us. We desperately needed a place to stay, so we had to leave my grandmother's place.

So, my mom suggested that her uncles open a house for us. We would take care of my great-grandmother, and of course, they would pay the rent.

They agreed with the idea. They needed someone to care for their mother, as they were too busy to do that.

They agreed immediately; waiting for someone to take the burden away was like waiting. In two weeks, we had a place to call our own; it was nothing fancy. It was a simple house with two bedrooms. I would sleep with my great-grandmother in one and my mom and my brothers in the second room.

Living with our great-grandma wasn't easy. She forgot many things and, acting like a child sometimes, was stubborn. However, we were willing to sacrifice to stop depending on the rest of the family for survival. She was losing her mind, yes, but never her love.

She would wait for me to wake up and give me 100 kisses. She always had a smile on her face, the warmest hugs, and the nicest life stories.

Every time I was feeling sick, or I had a headache, or I was not feeling well, she would make me sit next to her; she would start stating phrases from the Koran and touch my head while praying. It's a spiritual healing that Muslims use to defeat evil eyes and sickness.

She would brush my hair every day, and while making braids, she would tell me stories about her life. She told me that while she was living in Brazil, she managed to raise nine kids, have seven miscarriages, and still stand strong.

She liked being independent, dancing at weddings, cooking, and walking freely without explaining to any man. She opened a Lebanese restaurant in Brazil. It went well, but my great-grandfather didn't want to stay there. He wanted to go back to Lebanon, and he did leave her alone in Brazil.

He warned her that if she didn't return to Lebanon, he wouldn't divorce her but remarry again. She didn't believe him. After a few months, he called her, saying he had found someone else and was married. He built a house in Lebanon and lived there with his new wife.

The news killed her; she fell sick, and she couldn't work as before. Afterward, she returned to Lebanon to stay in that shoebox alone.

While her husband was with someone way younger than him in a huge house that was supposed to be hers, she told me while brushing my hair after showering, "Never give up anything for anyone. Everything you build is yours. People are selfish, and they will always put themselves first.

When you give up everything to be with someone, that person will never appreciate it. He will leave and continue with his life; you will be left alone and with nothing. It can be a husband, a family member, or anyone. Never leave behind your empire to help build someone else's."

I knew at that moment that she was hurt. She was talking about her husband, the one she had supported all her life, worked with, and made money with; eventually, he built a house with the money they made together, and he remarried a second wife younger than her, leaving her all alone in the dark.

I felt her pain, and I saved her wise words. The entire family gathered at one of my uncles' houses for lunch. He had a beautiful house with mountain views, a huge garden with chickens and ducks, beautiful flowers, and a breathtaking view.

After finishing lunch, I played with the twelve cats he had in his backyard and petted the cute, friendly ducks when I saw my brother Hamza running toward me.

He said he was eating cherries from the trees in the mountains when he heard dogs barking. He was too scared to leave alone, so he returned to the house. After a while, Ahmed, his best friend, showed up. We told him that some dogs might be in the mountains, and they were barking.

Ahmed suggested we climb there to play with the dogs, so we went. We climbed for about 15 minutes when we found a chicken farm, and many dogs guarded the chickens.

The dogs were so excited when they saw us. We started to play with them. They were waving their tails, jumping, and licking us; I was so happy to be there. I couldn't remember the last time I saw a dog; maybe it was in Colombia, and I was around 8 years old.

In small villages in Lebanon, it's not very common for people to have dogs in their houses. In Islam, if a dog's saliva touches your skin, you must wash yourself all over again to perform the prayers, and this is why it is rare for Muslims who follow the religion to raise dogs in their houses.

We heard a man screaming while we were playing with the dogs and making them chase us with their happy smiles and tails wagging. He was walking towards us with an angry face and shouting at us, telling us to leave his premises and not to touch the dogs. We were terrified of him.

So, we started to run back to the house; we didn't stop for a minute because we were scared that the guy was chasing us.

We arrived at my uncle's house out of breath, and after we put ourselves together, we started to laugh nonstop about the whole situation, making fun of Hamza's terrified face and the way Ahmed was running with his legs open. It was such a nice day for us kids at that time.

The next morning, I woke up late for school. I was rushing, and my great-grandmother stopped me to give me her hundred kisses. In the village, they don't care about you. They won't let you in if you arrive at school late. They close the door in your face. Hamza and I managed to make it on time.

I was so excited. I wanted to tell all my friends about the dogs in the mountains and what happened to us the previous day, but something was very wrong. I felt weird. My girlfriends ran away from me whenever I tried to interact with them. They would say a word or two and then leave me alone.

They ignored and excluded me. We got to class; we had two hours of mathematics that day. When she entered the class, the teacher asked if we had done our homework.

I didn't do it; I completely forgot about it. When she came to check, I told her that my homework wasn't done because I had forgotten. I had no excuse.

Back then, if you misbehaved at school, didn't do your homework, disrespected the teachers, or didn't say what they wanted to hear, they would make you open your hands and beat you in the palm of your hand with a piece of solid wood, and this is what happened to me.

She didn't care about me telling her the truth; she wouldn't forgive my irresponsibility for not completing that homework. She made me stretch my arms and open my hands with my palms facing up, and she hit me with a piece of solid, thick wood.

My hands were swollen, red, and burning; I could see a green vein coming out and hurting me.

The teacher said if I had done my homework, she wouldn't have beaten me; then I heard one of my classmates who was just seated behind me say, "She was too busy sucking dicks in the mountains." I heard what he said. Even though he said it whispering, I still heard him.

I turned to him, and I screamed in front of the entire class while still in pain, "Excuse me, repeat what you said just right now."

He was surprised. I think he didn't expect my reaction or didn't expect me to hear him. He said that this was what the entire school was talking about, that I was up in the mountains with a bunch of guys having sex with them. I couldn't believe what I was hearing.

This is why all my girlfriends wouldn't talk to me. Even the teacher was looking at me with a disgusted face. I looked at one of my closest friends and asked her if she believed in that and if she believed that I would do such a thing.

She said she didn't know what to believe and that her aunt, the school principal, had forbidden her to talk to me. The entire classroom looked at me with pity and disgust. I grabbed my things and ran away. I left school and ran towards home.

My legs were shaking, my breath was heavy, and my hands were painful and shaking, but I had to go home and tell my mom everything that was going on. All of this was a misunderstanding. All I was doing was petting and playing with the dogs. There were many cars parked outside of our house.

I immediately thought that something must have happened to my great-grandmother. Maybe she passed away, and that's why everybody was at our house. When I entered the living room, I saw my great-grandmother sitting there.

I was relieved, but when I looked to the right, I noticed that same old grumpy man from the farm shouting at us. All my uncles were there. My mom was seated next to her grandma with her eyes red; she had been crying; it was obvious.

"Nesrin, this man says you were at his farm with some men. Is that true?" said one of my uncles.

I was shocked. My vision was blurred, and I felt disoriented. I was so nervous that I thought the oxygen wasn't reaching my brain. I tried to hold back my tears and find the words to explain myself in front of the entire family and that old, grumpy man. "I wasn't with some man."

I was with Hamza and Ahmed, petting and playing with the dogs. You can just ask Hamza and Ahmed. They will prove to you that I'm not lying." The grumpy man jumps and starts shouting at me in front of everybody.

"Listen, girl, you shouldn't be hanging around farms, and climbing mountains is not for girls; you should be in the house helping your family with cooking and cleaning and not in the wild, and I hope your uncles give you a lesson.

Otherwise, you'll grow up and give them a lot of headaches." The grumpy man left our house, and my uncles stayed, advising me on how to be a lady. They said there were things that I could not do because they could destroy the family's reputation.

And if I'm not careful with my actions, nobody will want to marry me when I grow up. I told them I was sorry with my eyes swollen from crying and didn't mean to shame the family. It was an innocent mistake. I didn't think about the consequences.

Thanks to the grumpy man, I also told them about everything that happened at school and the horrible rumors people were spreading about me.

My mum was horrified with it; she told my uncles that I was just a child. How can people make rumors like this about a child? They asked her to rest the case because there was nothing they could do to erase the rumors and for her to pray for when the time for me to get married arrived.

Nobody remembers this tragic shame. When my uncles left the house, my mom told me to get ready because we were going back to school, and she would talk to the principal.

She was angry, and she said that the principal had no right to instruct the girls not to talk to me or to help with defamation and false accusations about a child. I was only a twelve-year-old kid dealing with horrific rumors.

When we arrived at school and entered the principal's office, my mom didn't even say hello to her; she asked her straight away with a very strict and angry tone of voice, "Are you brainwashing girls to not talk to my daughter due to rumors that came out that you know are not true?".

The principal told my mom she was not there to judge anyone, but the school had a standard and a reputation to keep, and I did not fit in that category. She mentioned that I was different from all the girls in the school. I didn't act like a normal girl but like a wild child.

I'm always running around, jumping, and talking to the guys. Last time, she even saw me playing football in the school backyard instead of being at painting class like all the other girls. She told Mom that she needed to protect the school's reputation and her niece's reputation as well.

Rumors spread fast about me being in the mountains with men, and some mothers called the school demanding not to see me near any of their daughters. That's why the girls were instructed not to talk to me anymore.

The principal finished her comments by saying, "Wild is in your daughter's name already, not only in her personality. If she cannot control that, she shouldn't be here."

My mom looked at her up and down, got closer, and hit her with, "I am sure if I was living in a castle, driving a Jeep, and had my wallet full of money, you wouldn't be standing here in front of me talking like this about my daughter; you would be defending her, but because we don't come from money, we don't get the respect.

My daughter will be transferred to another school so your students can be safe."

I was happy and relieved after seeing how my mom defended me.

She knew me; she knew everything was a lie. She didn't need to ask my brother if I was really with him because she always knew what she had raised. She knew I was being a child, doing what a child was supposed to do at my age: playing! Without any restrictions, rules, or worries about what people would do.

On our way out of the school, I asked her why the principal said Wild was in my name. She said, "Because your name is Nesrin, which means wild rose."

CHAPTER 4

A Shooting Star

شهاب

I woke up in the morning, and I found the bed full of blood; my great-grandmother was bleeding from her nose. I started to scream and immediately called my mom. We tried to stop the bleeding, making her lean forward, pinching her nose, and supporting it with napkins, but it was too much. So, we had to call an ambulance, and she was taken to the hospital.

That was the last time I saw her and the last memory I had of her alive. They tried to contain the bleeding with medication at the hospital, but in the end, she had a cardiac arrest and died there.

"Wake up, she is gone, wake up, she is gone," my mother screamed and cried when she answered a call from one of her uncles stating her grandma had passed away. It took me some time to put the pieces together; I only realized she was referring to my great-grandma when my mother was kneeling on the floor, sobbing and pleading for her grandmother's spirit to reach rest. I was heartbroken; I hadn't expected her to pass; it was only a nosebleed. She would definitely come home healthy and ready to start hugging and kissing us as usual.

I opened her closet, hugged all her dresses, smelled them, and cried, lying on top of them in the bed. The only person who understood me was gone. Who was going to give me a thousand kisses in the morning? Brush my hair? Remove all the evil eyes from me with her prayers? She was gone, and all that was left was her clothes in the closet and the stories she had told me. In Islam, we bury the dead straight away, so her funeral was the same day she passed.

The family started preparing the house for the funeral; neighbors brought coffee, food, and chairs. A ritual called Ghusull must be performed; it requires washing and shrouding the deceased before burial, and it is one of the religious obligations that must be carried out after death. Any older volunteer Muslim can do it, or it can be a member of the family, a neighbor, or a nurse. I remember her body arriving in the ambulance from the hospital, and some ladies came to start the Ghusull ritual on her in our backyard, which was located behind the kitchen. Kids are usually not allowed to be around or to watch, but I wanted to see her one last time and be by her side until her burial. There was a small window in the kitchen. I opened it slightly without anyone noticing, and I hid under that window, watching her lying down there with cotton inside her nose entrance and ears. I hid in the kitchen and watched the entire ritual through the window. I saw the religious ladies washing her body, praying on top of it, and stating the Quran's verses.

In Islam, it is said that what dies is the body; the soul of the person will still be around the house for 40 days. The dead will hear whatever you say out loud or in your head. They can hear the prayers. They can hear the worries. They can hear the cries. I knew that whatever I said, she would hear me. So, while they were washing her, I said, crying, with my hands on my chest and whispering into the air, "May your soul find peace; may you be in a better place than this. Don't abandon me; please visit me in my dreams.

I'm going to be so lost without you. Look after me and guide me to the right path wherever you are. I already miss you, and I love you."

Days passed; the house was empty without her. We were still healing. Trying to get used to the fact that she wasn't around anymore. It was painful. It was hard, but we also understood that she was old, and that's part of life. We are not immortal, but saying goodbye is never easy, especially when it is unexpected. For days, we kept hearing knocks on the doors; we would open, and no one was there. There was always a strong smell of alcohol in every corner of the house, and we wouldn't know where it was coming from. My mom started to sleep by my side in the bedroom, and the boys had the second bedroom for themselves.

One night, we were talking in bed, Mama and I, remembering a few moments with our grandma; she was telling stories about how she was always by her side when she delivered us in Brazil and how she used to love dancing at Arabic weddings barefoot, with a jar on her head, making Arabic moves with her hands, shaking her hips in every family wedding. That was a part of my great-grandma that I never knew. She was going to share this other side of her while brushing my hair, but we never had the chance. We almost fell asleep when we heard someone walking in the corridor; we thought it was one of my brothers. Then I saw the door handle moving up and down as if someone was trying to open it, but it didn't open. My mom stood up and opened the door; no one was there. She went to my brother's room, and they were both in deep sleep. She came back, looked at me, and asked, "Did you hear the door?" She said with both her eyes wide open and with a terrorized face. "I heard it and saw the door handle moving down as if someone was trying to enter the room."

She stood there frozen, not understanding what had just happened. I was sure that all the knocks and the alcohol smell were our grandma's soul roaming around the house, but I didn't want my mom to panic with my assumptions. The next day, my grandfather came to pay us a visit; of course, my mom told him everything that was going on inside the house. He reminded her that the soul of the dead roams the house for 40 days, but there is nothing to be afraid of. All we had to do was play the Quran inside the house and pray for her grandma's soul to find peace and mercy. Grandpa said that he had good news to tell us. He and his brothers decided to continue paying our rent even though their mother was gone. It would be like compensation for all the time we took care of her until her last day on earth. My mom, brothers, and I immediately clapped and hugged each other. That was a gift coming from the angels above because we were still in a miserable situation.

My dad would barely ask and wouldn't send money. My mom was not working. It was difficult to find a job in that village if you were a woman. There were never opportunities for women to work. We still depended on donations and help from our family members to survive. I would pray every day for our situation to change, for us to have a comfortable life, and for me to have the things I always dreamt about. I never went shopping for clothes because there was never enough money for that. I was still wearing my cousin's old clothes; whatever they didn't want, they would pass to me, and this was our life, a daily struggle. I would stand by the balcony waiting for a shooting star to pass because I believed it would come true if I spotted a shooting star and made a wish.

There I was, every night, looking at the sky, waiting for a sign, waiting for something bright to make that wish that, I believed, would change our life, until one night, it happened. I was with my mom on the balcony, and we were looking at the stars; she was smoking her cigarette, we were talking about regular things in life, and we both saw something bright passing on top of us very fast; immediately, I closed my eyes, and I made my wish. I still remember the wish for "money, a comfortable life, and a love to last."

When I opened my eyes, the sky was bright; it lit up the entire village, and I heard a huge explosive sound. I felt a wave of hot air in my face and the strong wind blowing away my mom and me. All the windows in the house were breaking. We were screaming. The neighbors were screaming. I was on the ground. My mom grabbed me from my T-shirt, and she pulled me up, and she said, "It's a bomb run, it's a bomb."

My mom grabbed my brothers and me, and we ran to the streets because we were scared that the house would fall on us. The electricity in the entire village was cut off. We were bending down and hiding behind a wall in the streets, and many people were doing the same. I could see my mom's hand. She was shaking. I was scared. We were all scared and did not understand what was happening. I could hear babies crying and kids crying. People screaming. The sound of the sirens of the ambulances. We stayed in the streets, bending down for at least an hour, until everything calmed down, and then we returned home. We entered the house, which was almost destroyed from the inside. The glasses were everywhere on the floor, dust, and everything was dark.

Then, we came to know that Lebanon was under attack by the Israeli army. A war was about to start, and we were caught in the middle of it. That night, nobody slept. Even after not hearing anything, we were terrified. My mom was hugging me while I was crying. I had never encountered a war before, never heard a bomb, and never had this hopeless feeling of dying at any minute. We stayed awake cleaning the glasses and worried that another bomb would fall above us. It had already been a week since the war started in the south of Lebanon. Our village was in the west in the countryside, but we were getting attacked because the Muslim Shias from the south were coming to hide in our villages, and Israel wanted to get them all. We opened our village schools to accommodate those who had lost their houses and those who had to flee the south to survive. I still remember Israel sending drones.

We were terrified of them, and we would switch off all the lights in the houses, streets, and everywhere so they would think there was no one there. We would sleep with our clothes on because in case they send a bomb, we have time to run. The windows were always open to avoid them breaking like the last time. I often had nightmares that the house was falling on us or that an Israeli soldier was invading our house and shooting all of us. Even when I was awake, any sound would make me scream and shake. It didn't matter where the attack was happening or where the bombs were falling; we could still hear the explosions, and the house would shake as if there was an earthquake. At some point, I was glad my great-grandma wasn't alive. She was old, wouldn't handle a war, wouldn't even be able to run, and would get hurt.

My dad finally called to check on us, but I don't remember when I heard his voice. He was worried and wanted us out of there. He said the Brazilian government was sending governmental aircraft with the Brazilian army to rescue its people who were stuck in Lebanon. Still, my mom said she would never leave Lebanon and her family behind. My mom's entire family holds a Brazilian passport, and yet, none of them wanted to leave the country; they would say running away is for cowards; they would never leave their homes or their lands for Israel to steal or occupy.

I begged Mom for us to leave. My brothers and I were scared, terrified, and having nightmares, and we would scream and run to the streets every time there was an explosion nearby, and the house started to shake. My parents spent hours talking on the phone until they agreed to send Walid with the Brazilian government to be close to my dad; he was 18 years old and could travel alone. Hamza and I were underage, and we stayed in the middle of the war with my mom. Everything was so fast in two days; Walid's approval to board the military plane arrived, and he had to leave Lebanon immediately. We had no time to talk; my brother cried so much. He didn't want to leave without us, but at least someone from the family could be saved. I know it was a hard and harsh decision for my parents to separate us, but the circumstances back then were abnormal. Walid hugged me tight, and he was crying.

"We will see each other again. I will always call you, and I promise you."

I didn't say anything; I didn't reply to him; I was crying so much that I was running out of breath, and I was angry with everything and everyone around me. My mom received a call from Aunt Fatima saying that she also got accepted to escape Lebanon in the Brazilian military planes, and they were both going to stay with my dad. Another person I loved was leaving, escaping, and we were staying in a country falling apart, with empty houses and broken windows. They were both going to reunite with my dad, the person I missed the most. They both left worried about us, with tears and remorse for leaving us behind. But it was my family's choice not to leave. What was left for us was to accept the reality that we were living in a war and pray every day to stay alive.

Lebanon was receiving donations from all over the world. Uncle Mosab was the head of the Muslim group of scouts, and he called me to work with him and help organize donations worldwide. I was only 14 years old, managing and supervising a group of people, instructing them how to organize the donations, separate cans of food, and where to deliver them. That was my job for the entire time until the war was over. Not what a normal teenager would be doing in another part of the world. They would go to school, dream of a future, and hug their loved ones. Our reality was different. Our schools were being used for the people who had lost their homes, our friends were getting buried, and our loved ones were escaping the war.

The war lasted for over a month, and it was enough time to destroy the south of Lebanon completely and a big part of Beirut. Thousands of innocent people were killed most brutally, most of them kids. There were still many people trapped under the ruins, some of them alive, some of them were alive but weren't saved on time.

The stress, the fear, and the anxiety were over, but the sadness and the heartbreak for those who didn't make it were painful. The war was over, but not the traumas. The sleepless nights. The nightmares. The scars of living in fear. Those were things we carried with us for the rest of our lives. An experience or an event that nobody should deserve to live or feel. For a long time, I kept having vivid dreams about war and would often wake up the entire house screaming. I would dream about being chased by drones, being attacked by soldiers, or watching buildings fall to the ground in front of me. It wasn't the way I pictured my childhood to be, but it was something I learned to deal with.

CHAPTER 5
The Hardest Goodbye
أصعب وداع

T hree years had passed since the war in Lebanon ended. Many things happened in our lives. My mom started selling a popular Brazilian snack called coxinha—crispy, teardrop-shaped dough filled with seasoned shredded chicken. She would make hundreds of them and sell them frozen to the supermarkets in the village.

It was a bold move for her—at the time, it was rare for women in the village to work, and opportunities for them to grow professionally were almost nonexistent. The only women I would see working were the hairdressers in the salons, and there was just one female doctor and one nurse.

You would never see a woman becoming a mayor, a lawyer, an ambassador, or even a school van driver. Those roles men always occupied them. The women were mostly stay-at-home wives, sending the kids to school, cooking, cleaning, and looking pretty.

My mom was tired of depending on her parents for money. She wanted to give us a better life, and the only thing she was taught to do was cook. She was exceptional at cooking Brazilian food and pastries. All the supermarkets in the village were buying from her, but everything good and shining there would eventually be destroyed.

People started to report fake news about getting food poisoning from her food; the news was spreading fast in the village, saying she was not clean, some of them would say her food could not be consumed, and even pictures with human hair inside her pastries were shared until the grocery stores stopped buying from her.

She was devastated; I could see her crying every night and saying how much she hated that place and regretted not leaving when she had the chance to leave when Brazil sent the rescue planes during the war. We always tried to cheer her up, but it never worked. She wouldn't stand up for herself and clear the rumors.

Despite her unwavering determination to protect our family, it seemed as though she had given up on advocating for her rights. A few weeks later, we learned that it was all a set-up by another miserable woman in the village who spread the rumors about my mom's food being poisonous and planted hair in the food on purpose so she could take my mom's place and start selling the same Brazilian food to the supermarkets.

Walid was in São Paulo, living with my dad and Auntie Fatima. He was studying and working, always calling to check on us and sending me money to buy the things I wanted. Hamza was never home, always out with his friends, and always with money in his pockets that I had no idea where he was getting it from, and I? I was in love.

I developed a huge crush on Amer. I knew everything about him—from where he lived and went to school to his zodiac sign and even his parents' names. I was constantly finding out more, asking questions, and doing everything I could to make sure he noticed me.

I saw him only at village gatherings and weddings. I would wake up earlier for school and wait for his van ahead of time to see him for two seconds as his school vehicle passed in front of my house. I even knew what time it would pass.

I wasn't spending the money that Walid was sending me on clothes or shopping. I was saving it to buy a computer. All my friends at school had computers and the internet, but my parents could never afford to buy me one. Whenever there was a school project, I had to go to someone's house to study with them, and I always came up with the excuse of "My computer is under maintenance" because I was too ashamed to say that I didn't own one.

I managed to save $300 with the little money that Walid would send me monthly. I bought my computer, installed the internet, and created my first MSN account and a Facebook page. I went straight away to look for Amer's profile and add him as a friend on Facebook.

He accepted my friend request the next day, added me on MSN, and started chatting. He started the conversation, and my heart was beating fast; I couldn't believe I was finally chatting with my crush. I stalked him for two years and would dress up pretty for every event that I knew he was going to be there to get his attention, but he never made a move; he was always in his own space with his friends, but in the chat, he said that he knew me and that he would always see me around and that in his eyes, I was the prettiest girl in that village.

We talked for hours, but we both had to go because we had school the next morning. Before we ended the conversation, he said he needed to tell me something: "Your green eyes are pretty."

When I read that, I ran out of breath; he always noticed me, he knew who I was, and the same way I would gather information about him, he would do the same about me; we didn't know how to get close or reach each other, and that's how our love story began.

Back in the day and still until today, girls are not allowed to meet with guys without being engaged or without their parents' permission. We were not allowed to date or hold hands in public. If a girl were caught meeting with a guy in secret, she would be in big trouble; the whole village would picture her as a whore, make up stories, and no man would marry her.

Of course, this judgment was never applied to the man. The bad reputation would follow the girl for the rest of her life. She would be considered a sinner or someone not suitable for marriage. I grew up hearing the same quote over and over from the elders in my family: "The man who wants a girl will walk through the door to ask for her hand, and not through the window."

الشاب يلي بدو البنت بفوت من الباب،
و مش من الشباك

In their minds, if the guy loved the girl, he had to go through the entrance door and ask for permission from her parents to get to know her. If he kept her a secret and asked her to meet in hidden places, it meant he was not serious about marriage and only wanted to take advantage of a girl.

Amer and I had to be careful; we would never meet secretly. We spent hours talking online and on the phone when our parents were sleeping, but we never met face to face. We would only see each other from far away. He would pass by my house with his car, and I would stand by the balcony to see him from far away. That was the only way to keep me safe from people's mouths.

We kept doing that for a whole year; we were deeply in love, even without ever touching me or kissing me. One morning, my mom called Hamza and me to talk in the living room; she said she had something very important to discuss with us. I felt her nervous, and she had watery eyes.

She started by saying:

"Life in Lebanon hasn't been easy for me. We moved here because your dad and I wanted you to learn Arabic and the culture, meet the whole family, and follow the traditions and the religion. We were scared we would lose you to the outside world, and back then, that was the best decision for our family.

I understand your dad disappeared for a while and didn't send money. We have been facing difficulties for years, and he regrets it. Now, it's time for us to be a family again. I'm here to tell you it's time to move to Brazil and reunite with your father and brother.

I have spoken to your dad, and he will issue us tickets next week. We will sell everything and start a new life."

Hamza stood up screaming and shouting, saying he would not leave Lebanon. He loved it there and said she was only doing this because of the rumors people made about her food and destroying her business. Screaming and angry, he said, "I'm not leaving Lebanon, especially now that I'm finally making money and opening my own business."

My mom stood with her arms crossed, looking at him, and asked, "What money?" She looked at me, and I moved my head from left to right, showing her I also had no idea what he was talking about. Honestly, I didn't care; I was still shocked by the news. Hamza left the living room crying and banging all the doors behind him. Tears were falling down my face.

"Why are you crying? You never liked this place anyway; did you forget everything they did to you when you were just a child? Or the sleepless nights during the war?"

I told her many things changed, and I would rather not leave anymore. I had learned how to survive in that village where nothing ever happened. I made new friends and learned how to play by the rules and obey them. But then she reminded me of what they had done to destroy her business; she was mentally tired of everything we had been through: the poverty, the nonstop rumors, the way people would look down on us for not being rich, and the disrespect. My mother wanted a fresh start next to her husband and her son; she wanted us to be all together again.

I understood her point.

It was a toxic village with rotten people. A place with no future, only families being destroyed, girls having arranged marriages, and people interfering in other people's lives. I stood up quietly and went back to my room. I needed the space to process everything that was going on.

I went straight online to talk to Amer. I told him everything that was going on; my hands were shaking while typing, my chest was completely red from anxiety, he got very upset with the news, he didn't want me to leave, and at the same time, he said it's not fair for me to stay because of him and leave my family behind.

We made a video chat, cried together, spoke for hours as usual, and tried to find a way out of this mess.

"What if you tell your parents that Brazil isn't the right place for you as a Muslim girl? It's a different culture and different people, and they will be worried about you all the time; tell them that the place is not suitable for a girl like you and that Lebanon is where a family girl should be raised.

You stay with your grandparents, finish school here, and we don't have to be away from each other."

This was Amer's plan, and I agreed to it. I came out of my room; my mom was still in the living room, with her Arabic coffee, a cigarette, and swollen eyes. I told her exactly what Amer told me to say, and she said

"I was born in Brazil; I was raised there. Brazil will not take you on the wrong path because you know who you are and how we raised you. You are old enough to know what's halal and what's haram. We will all go back together, like we raised you here, and we will continue doing it there."

She seemed very determined in her decision, and nothing would make her change her mind about leaving. Our plan failed; nothing I said would make her change her decision. A part of me wanted to leave that village and see my dad and brother, and another part wanted to stay with my cousins, friends, and the love of my life.

I returned online and told Amer that our plan didn't work and we were leaving Lebanon next week. He said he would not allow that to happen and had another thing in mind, but he would only tell me tomorrow because it involved other people. I knew exactly his other plan: he would talk to his parents and propose to me.

When a man proposes to a girl, that girl automatically becomes his responsibility, so I would have to stay in Lebanon close to my fiancé until the marriage. I jumped from happiness; my biggest dream was to be his wife. I loved him and was dying to be part of his family.

I ended the chat with him and called my cousin Rayan immediately, and she confirmed that he would propose. We were both screaming with happiness because I wasn't leaving anymore. I would stay close to her and marry the love of my life. We were already imagining what the wedding would be like and what kind of engagement ring I would choose.

The wedding guest list and the type of wedding dress I would wear were all part of a fairy tale.

I woke up super early the next morning, singing, and I started to clean the house because he would surely come with his parents to ask for my hand. I took a bucket with water and soap and started scrubbing the walls, dusting, rearranging a few pieces of furniture, and leaving everything shining to receive my future family.

When I finished all the cleaning, I went online to talk to him. He was online, and I asked him if he worked on plan B and spoke to the other people he would involve, and he said.

"I'm sorry, Nesrin. It will not work out. You need to leave to be with your family."

I couldn't believe what I was reading; he was breaking up with me. Yesterday, we were talking, and he would fight the world for me, and the next day, I was being dumped. It took me a few minutes to process what he said, and I read it multiple times before I texted him back.

"Are you breaking up with me? I thought you would propose to me and not let me leave!"

"I am not breaking up with you; we were never serious. I never asked you to be my girlfriend. We were just together, and I thought you already knew I never said I would propose to you; we would never work. We are just friends who love each other; I never mentioned that I would ever marry you.

I love you, yes, but I never planned a future with you or made you promises; we would never work out. We come from different social backgrounds. Your family is having trouble, and your reputation is not the best. My family comes from a high society, which is not a good match."

I read his message over and over for at least 20 minutes; I couldn't answer him; I couldn't breathe. This means he never took me seriously; just because his family comes from money and mine is humble, I wasn't good enough? Or did he love me but was ashamed of me and my family because we were poor, never owned a car or land, and lived in a simple house? We did not meet his family standards, and his parents would never accept their son marrying a girl who had lived all her life waiting for clothes donations and had never left the village because her parents never even had money to afford a family day out.

I was devastated; everything was so blurred. I locked myself in the toilet, and I was crying, and it was getting out of control. I looked at myself in the mirror. My eyes were so small from crying, and my chest and ears were red. I never answered him back.

I heard the doorbell ring. I stood straight away and washed my face, trying to pull myself back together. For a second, I thought it might be Amer by the door. Maybe he would say that it was all a joke, a misunderstanding, and that he didn't mean what he said.

Maybe he's by the door now to end this nightmare and tell me he loves me and wants to spend the rest of his life with me. I came out of the toilet, and a man in the living room was talking to my mom; she seemed furious and apologized nonstop to the man.

Then I saw Hamza seated in the corner, crying. I didn't understand what was happening, so I waited for the man to leave and get the full story. It turned out that the man came to complain to my mom about Hamza; he was visiting a land he had in the mountains and caught Hamza picking cherries from his 22 trees and emptying them into bags.

It turned out that Hamza's gold business was going to people's premises, emptying their trees of cherries, apples, and even almonds. He would sell the fruits to supermarkets in the village for a very attractive cheap price, and he wasn't alone. He would pay his friends to help with the job.

When the man left, my mom lost it and started to scream at him. She said she couldn't handle being attacked by the people in the village over and over again.

"Our reputation is on the floor; nobody respects us, and they never will. WE ARE LEAVING."

She kept saying it, screaming and crying. There was no more arguing; we were leaving that country for good, and it's not up to us to decide that anymore. I looked at her with my crying, swollen eyes and told her, "Let's leave; we don't belong here."

I don't remember how it all happened; everything was so fast. We had our bags ready within days, and it felt like we were running away from the bad guys. The desperation of leaving that village and all our traumas behind was so great that we didn't have much time to say goodbye to many people.

The only thing that I remember is that it hurt a lot; it was one of the hardest goodbyes I have ever had in my entire life. All my cousins were with us on the way to the airport. Rayan was crying, and she kept repeatedly saying how her life would be miserable with me gone.

We had a strong bond. She was the first face I saw when we arrived in Lebanon and the last one I saw when we left. She gave me a paper with a handwritten quote from the Koran. She told me that whenever I feel anxious, lost, tired, or like I'm waiting for something to become true, I just read it.

It's a quote called "Ayat Al Kursi," and the powerful quote would bring peace to my soul and happiness to my heart. I thanked her for the sweet gesture, folded the paper gently, put it in my purse, leaned my head on her shoulder, and kept playing in my mind all the good memories I had there and the bad ones.

How could I forget the pajama nights with my cousins, the midnight secrets with Rayan, the family picnics, the laughs, the crying, me wearing used clothes every Eid, my mom selling all her gold to pay our school fees, the flowers blooming when it was springtime and us lying on the grass dreaming about who we would marry, going up the hill with my cousins to watch the sunset, the times my great grandma was alive and giving me all the life advice, the war and all the panic, everything we had lost and everything we had gained living there?

It was like a movie playing in my head, but I knew we didn't belong there. If freedom, independence, and growth were what I sought, then it was time to leave, even if it hurt. My heart was bleeding, but my soul was craving the change.

We would go somewhere new now to start fresh. Somewhere, nobody knew us, nobody would judge us, and no one cared about reputation or social status. Somewhere, I could play with dogs, walk, ride a bike, and climb buildings without hearing, "That's not for ladies." Somewhere, men and women have the same rights—somewhere, I could finally be myself.

I don't remember being on the plane to Brazil; my memory is zero. The experience was so traumatic and painful that I have buried it somewhere in my mind. The only memory I have is Baba waiting for us at the airport, with Walid and me running to hug them.

CHAPTER 6

Her Dream Before Mine

حلمها قبل حلمي

When we got to our new São Paulo, Brazil, house, my dad and Aunt Fatima cleaned the whole house. Walid showed us the house's layout; it had two floors, a kitchen, a living room, a laundry room, and a barbecue downstairs; upstairs were the bedrooms, and for the first time in years, I had an entire bedroom for myself. My dad set aside a queen bed for me, a large closet, and some pink drapes. The boys shared a smaller bedroom, and the suite was for our parents.

My dad was doing better at his work, so he could afford to rent something to make us comfortable following all the years of hardships in Lebanon. The house was rather beautiful. I wanted to go downstairs to log in and tell Rayan about our new house and way of life. The computer ran on a password. Sitting beside me, Walid asked, "Guess the password?" I guessed several names and birth dates and found nothing correct. "Nesrin, the password is Nesrin; that's how much I missed you. I know you don't like to be called by your real name, but it's the prettiest for me."

I hugged Walid so tight that he said I was smashing him. I sent an offline message to my cousins saying how much I was missing them and updated them about how we arrived and about the house, and I sent pictures of my bedroom. That's how excited I was to finally have my private space.

Later that afternoon, my dad said there was a mall just 5 minutes away from our house and wanted to take us there. I had never been to a mall in my entire life. I was 17 years old, and the only mall I had seen was in movies. There were no such things in the village, and the closest mall was in Beirut, which was a two-hour drive. We never had money to buy anything or explore Lebanon, and I never had the opportunity to enter a mall. They took us there, and for the first time, I saw what I would only see on TV: all the stores, clothes, cinema, the smell of popcorn, a food court, the escalators, and the bright lights. We had some ice cream there, and I could see my mom's face; she was happy and relieved.

It was a different reality from what we were living. It was a completely new world, brimming with opportunities, people, and cuisine. I was at the mall, gazing around, and for a brief moment, I considered that I did not wish to be there. I nearly missed the opportunity to be with my family and visit places that I had never imagined I would visit because I was in love with a man who was ashamed of introducing me to the world.

Then I remembered everything my great grandma said when brushing my hair about never giving up on anything because of anyone. I felt grateful that my mom disagreed with me staying in Lebanon. She was right; we should stick together as a family. We went home at night, and Walid wanted to show me something on his computer; he promised it would be incredible. He opened YouTube, and we watched a video about how a neighborhood shaped like a palm was built on top of the water in Dubai. I didn't even know that there was a place called Dubai; Walid explained that it was in the Middle East, 3 hours away from Lebanon by plane, and it was one of the cities in the United Arab Emirates.

About fifty years ago, this country was completely built on top of the desert. I couldn't believe what I was seeing; there was too much information, and if I hadn't seen it with my own eyes, I wouldn't have believed it. The video described how they used sand to build The Palm on top of the ocean. My mother was amused, so I asked her to join us in watching it. After that, we began watching more videos that explained how Dubai was constructed and the Sheikhs' goal of making it one of the world's most opulent cities.

We stayed hours in front of the computer, learning about Dubai and the United Arab Emirates. He told me he was obsessed with the videos and was always watching what was coming new in that city. He showed me other videos about how Burj Khalifa, the tallest building in the world, was built and about the Burj Al Arab, the only hotel rated as a six-star hotel. We found an interview with a Brazilian reporter in the Middle East, who interviewed random people at the biggest mall in the world, the Dubai Mall. He asked one of the ladies what she does in Dubai. She said she was a flight attendant living in Dubai for two years and always goes to the Dubai Mall, but it's so big that she hasn't explored it all yet.

I was shocked; I imagined the amount of money in that country, with the vision and ambition those people had to start a whole country in the desert. I kept wondering how people survive living there. It must be a very expensive city to live in. Walid explained that most jobs in Dubai provide accommodation for their employees; he guessed that the girl in the interview who said she was a flight attendant most probably works for Dubai Airways, a successful airline based in Dubai that offers accommodation to all their employees. My mom joins the conversation and says, "This girl is everything I wanted to be; she's living my teenage dream."

Walid and I kept looking at her without understanding, and she continued, "When I was young, my biggest dream was to become a flight attendant, but I couldn't. I would sit outside our house here in São Paulo and watch the planes pass in the skies. Sometimes, I would race to see who was faster; your grandfather would shout and make me go inside the house. I think I was around 14 years old."

I never knew this about her; my mom never told us about her life before meeting my dad. I would have never expected her to have this dream of wanting to become a flight attendant. She said that it was every girl's dream back in the day. It was like a flight attendant hype. My grandfather traveled a lot in Brazil, and she would always go with him. Even though she was still young, she kept staring at the flight attendants every time they traveled, wishing to be like them one day. Then I remembered on the plane from Colombia to Lebanon when I told that flight attendant I wanted to be like her someday; this memory just came into my head. I buried it for years, and something inside of me also wanted to have this life. I asked my mom if this was a big dream for her and why she didn't make it true. Mama said she never had the choice of being what she wanted and never had control over her life or future. She knew it was only a dream and that making it come true was impossible, but then she took a deep breath and said she would tell me everything about it the next morning over coffee.

She left to sit beside my dad to watch TV, and I asked Walid to tell me more about Dubai Airways. Something was awakened inside me; I was curious and wanted to know everything about the job and the company. I had so many questions, like, how do you become a flight attendant? Do you need to be pretty? Skinny? Speak many languages? Have a visa? Have a passport? Be tall? Look like a model? How much is their salary?

"Calm down, lady. I don't know how to answer all your questions or what is needed to become a flight attendant, but we can do some digging together, " said Walid, trying to make me relax and calm my anxiousness.

First, we started by visiting the Dubai Airways website because there would be all my unanswered questions and doubts. There was an option called "Join our team." He pressed the flight attendant section, and a brand-new page opened with the faces of their flight attendants, wearing that brown uniform, with their big white teeth smiling and that charming red lipstick, and under their picture, it was written, "Let's discover the tomorrow together."

"Imagine how crazy it would be to travel the whole world and still get paid for it."

That's what I told Walid with both my hands on my chest, not believing that someone out there is having this life, the life my mom dreamt of having, and thousands of women around the world, and I was becoming one of those dreamers too. We scrawled down the page, and it was written, "Join our international family of over 100 nationalities, be based in Dubai, with a tax-free salary, paid accommodation, and get to see the whole world while getting paid."

I asked Walid if that wasn't a fake advertisement or a scam because it was too good to be true. He explained to me that it wasn't a scam and that Dubai Airways was one of the fastest-growing airlines in the world. He also explained that not just the airlines pay for accommodation in Dubai for their employees; many other jobs, like hotels, taxi drivers, constructors, and restaurants, also do. They arrange everything for their employee: the visa, the medical benefits, the accommodation, and transportation to work.

I never thought a country could do so much for its expats and workers. All the information was overwhelming; the more positive things I heard, the more excited and anxious I became. We scrolled down a bit more and found the answers we had been seeking; the requirements to join the airline team as flight attendants were:

- *Age required: 21 years old and above.*

- *No visible tattoos while in uniform.*

- *Fluent in English (written and spoken).*

- *To be medically fit and healthy.*

- *A minimum of a high school diploma is required; any university degree or course would be a plus.*

- *The minimum accepted height is 1.65 cm.*

"Of course, you don't have tattoos. It is haram; you are fluent in English thanks to your good education in Lebanon. Your height is 1.70 cm. You are medically fit and have a healthy weight. What is missing here is you finishing high school, then waiting three and a half years more until you turn 21; then you will be ready to become a Dubai Airways flight attendant if Dad allows you, and if you don't end up getting an arranged marriage before you turn 21." Said Walid, looking at me with his sarcastic smile.

That was much time to wait; many things could happen in those 3 years, and as Walid said, I could end up like my mom, married and forbidden to follow a dream. My dad would not accept the idea of me moving abroad by myself. Not getting married. Live a single and independent life as the foreigners do. Traveling by myself without a family member present. Baba would not digest all this information, especially with our cultural beliefs and background, where women are not allowed to be more than home-makers.

In 3 years, many things could go wrong or right. It could be enough time to convince Baba slowly to allow me to live the flight attendant dream, or it would be enough time for my family to find a decent guy for me to marry. The future was a mystery, scaring me, but I had to take things like baby steps. I had many things to focus on, and many things around me were changing. I didn't know how to speak Portuguese properly; I had the challenge of learning a new language, understanding a new culture, and adapting to this new life.

The next morning, I found my mom seated outside in the barbeque area, like always, drinking her Arabic coffee and the cigarette in her hand. I told her about Walid and Googled about flight attendant life and the airline in Dubai. All this information made me want to live that life, too. The life of getting paid for traveling, sleeping in hotels, and living in the most luxurious city in the world. I want that for myself, too, but I'm too young, so I might have to wait a few years.

"I know that you want it too. We all do; we all did. Every woman you meet will tell you the same thing: that she has always wanted to be a flight attendant. But sometimes those dreams end up being just wishes."

Said my mom with a soft and low voice. I could see sadness in her eyes when she spoke about this subject. It was a subject that brought her a lot of pain and disappointment. I never knew anything about her past, about her life before she had her kids. I didn't even know how she met my father, how things happened, how we were born in Brazil, and how we ended up in Colombia. Suppose my dad's part of the family treated her right if her marriage was arranged and if that was the life she chose for herself. I never asked her, and she never opened the subject while I was growing up. I asked my mom, "Do you mind if I grab a coffee and you tell me your story?". "What story?" she said.

"The story about your dream before mine," I replied.

CHAPTER 7

Zhur

زهور

*I*f you believe you were misunderstood in your childhood, it is because you haven't heard the story of my childhood. My dad named me Zhur after your great-grandmother. It means flowers in Arabic, but I was no flower at all.

He migrated from Lebanon to Brazil as a teenager to live a better life. My four siblings and I were born in Brazil, yet we never had the freedom all Brazilians have.

He had a clothing store doing very well; he was a very successful businessman with a very strong and harsh personality. He was so overprotective; he was nothing compared to your dad.

We were never allowed to leave the house if he wasn't with us, and we couldn't even sit by the stairs in front of the house without an adult present. He had this huge fear of us losing ourselves, our culture, and our beliefs to the foreign world.

We were all in school, but we had zero friends. No friends were allowed to come into our house, and we were not allowed to visit them. After school, we would go home straight away, and if we got delayed and he figured out, he would beat us up.

My father would always take us along when he traveled to see relatives in distant Brazilian states or to purchase merchandise for his store. My desire to work as a flight attendant began like this.

When I saw all those attractive women in uniform, grinning and lugging their bags through the airport, I wished I were one of them.

For hours, I would wait outside my bedroom window for airplanes to fly past, thinking of them as shooting stars, and I would always make a wish. Despite having a long list of things I wanted, I never fulfilled them.

Additionally, I kept my dream a secret from all of your aunts. Every time they spoke it in front of my grandfather, I feared I would be punished for wanting something I couldn't have.

The only time we would leave the house was when my father was at work; we would sneak out without him knowing; we would go to the mall to buy ice creams and come back running before someone saw us and told him.

I never sneaked outside the house to do anything wrong; I just wanted to do what a normal teenager my age would do: meet with friends, go for walks, shop, and buy ice cream with no fear.

But I knew that in his head, he would never believe I was getting an ice cream with my siblings or just walking to have some fresh air.

He would think I was meeting up with guys, and I would never have a chance to defend myself or speak up because he would hit me so hard before I spoke. I don't think that I was accepting and living by his rules; I wasn't.

I was always answering back to him, even after the slaps. I asked him why he was hating me when I hadn't done anything wrong.

I would question my mom, always asking why I could not do certain things or normal teenage things like all the other girls, but she would always tell me to shut up and respect my father.

I had a very strong personality and a wild attitude, and I wouldn't shut my mouth. He never used to give us money in our hands; everything was so controlled. If we needed something, we needed permission from him, even to buy a simple bag of chips.

I used to steal things from his clothing store, take them to school, and sell them there to make money.

That's how every year, I would buy my mom a gift on Mother's Day. Dressing up was my passion.

I was a very pretty girl, tall, blonde, skinny, with green eyes. With the money I used to make selling the stolen things from his store, I used to buy myself clothes when he was working and would lie that I got them as gifts from family members; it was the only way to live like a normal teenage girl.

I still remember one day when we went to spend a day with our family members on a farm; it was a private farm with no outsiders, only family.

I was not allowed to play with my male cousins, so we used to play and meet secretly when my father wasn't around. They were all swimming at a lake nearby, and I bought myself a swimsuit, put it on, and went swimming with them in the lake.

I thought your grandfather was far away from the farm. That's why I was so comfortable and confident playing with my cousins in the lake and wearing a swimsuit.

But he had changed his mind about the long trip and returned to the farm earlier, and he saw me there, with my legs showing, playing with my male cousins.

He grabbed me by my hair from the lake to the farmhouse, and he started to hit me with his belt.

I wanted to play with them and wear a bathing suit, even though I knew I was not supposed to, and I didn't see anything wrong with it. He beat me up in front of our entire family, and no one stopped him.

I was only eleven years old then, so I couldn't comprehend why it wasn't permitted. He pulled me out of school when I was 14 and told my mother that I should stay at home, learn how to cook, and get ready to be a decent housewife.

It annoyed me because I liked learning, did well academically, and intended to pursue a career in journalism before deciding to become a flight attendant.

For days, I begged my mother to let me finish school and not let this happen, claiming that Brazilian schools were unsafe for children my age.

I was aware that they secretly feared I would fall in love with a non-Muslim man, breach all the family's customs and rules, and cause them shame.

One day, my dad came home with our cousin's wedding videotape from Lebanon that was sent to him; he played it on the TV for us to watch.

Lebanese weddings are like fairy tales; the bride always has a big sparkling dress and full makeup, the whole village usually attends the wedding, and everybody dances "Dabke," the traditional Arab dance, and this is how I met your father.

He was dancing on that videotape and was very handsome and charming. The minute I saw him on the TV, I instantly had a crush on him and even told your aunties that this was the guy I would marry.

A few months passed, and our house in Lebanon was built.

My dad was rich and had bought a lot of land back home, built a house that looked like a castle, and told my mom it was time to leave Brazil because we were growing up, and he wanted to raise us among the Arab community.

We didn't speak much Arabic back then. It wasn't a hard goodbye leaving Brazil. I never had friends to say goodbye to. We barely left the house or had any social life, which was a part of our runaways when he was at work.

I was excited to leave; I had the same mentality as you. I told myself, "Maybe it will be a fresh start, and I will have more freedom." Being there around the family, our dad would trust us and let us go out anywhere we wanted, but he didn't.

Life in that village wasn't easy for us either. He didn't change his mentality; we were still not allowed to go out much, but at least I made friends.

I had a female Arabic tutor at home to teach me Arabic; I was still not allowed to wear what I wanted; it was way stricter there. Girls were not allowed to mix with men or have male friends.

I would mostly hang out with your aunt Fatima. Despite being your grandpa's sister, she was the youngest child, and our age difference was only 4 years. She was 18 years old, and I was 15.

She wasn't married yet, and it was unusual for a girl her age to be still single, but my grandmother didn't want her to get married to the first guy who would knock at her door; she was very protective of her and wanted her to have the best life, with a decent husband.

We always hung out at my grandfather's house; I would sit by the balcony with Aunt Fatima because I knew when your dad would go for his football match. Every time he passed, we would stare at each other.

I loved him but never spoke to him; it was not allowed. My time there wasn't easy; everyone envied me. I had very mean cousins who wouldn't leave me alone and would wish bad things on me.

My dad's older sister, Aunt Lamia, would fill up my dad's head with rumors about me, that I was always by the balcony and talking to guys, or that my clothes were too tight, and that the village was talking badly about me.

My dad would believe everything she told him, and he would beat me up without asking me if it was true.

Aunt Lamia used to hate me; she believed that I was there to steal future husbands from her daughters because I was pretty, young, and coming from abroad.

She saw me once by the balcony smiling at your father when he was passing by; she started to shout at me, calling me a whore, and stating that I was planning to steal her daughter's future husband.

That Khaled, your dad, was in love with her older daughter, and I was throwing myself at him to destroy their soon-to-be engagement. Of course, I didn't let her talk to me the way she wanted and invent lies about me.

I told her, screaming in her face, not to worry because I wasn't there to steal from anyone and that marriage wasn't my priority.

"I will not get married; I will become a flight attendant and live far away from you and this toxic family; you can keep the trophy for your daughter; I don't want it."

She started to laugh, a very loud laugh, as if she were a witch.

And she said that she expected me to have this kind of mentality of wanting to do something no well-raised girl would want to do because I didn't have what it takes to be a decent housewife or a respectable wife; she said this whore life suits me.

I knew she had told my dad from the way he parked the car and walked straight towards me, with his eyes wide open and his red face of anger; he kicked me, I fell on the floor, and he kept kicking me while I was on the floor, saying that no daughter of his would bring him any shame and destroy the family's reputation.

My whole body was bruised, and I was still in pain. Aunt Fatima came over and said she heard rumors that your dad never wanted any of Aunt Lamia's daughters.

She took her older daughter to their house for coffee, throwing her at him and forcing an engagement. I was happy and relieved because my love for him was bigger than anything.

A week later, your dad came over and proposed to me; our love story started there. We got engaged and had a huge engagement party; for the first time, I wore makeup. I was so pretty, and I could see the hate on my cousin's face.

I could hear all the whispers and rumors of "What did he see in her?" but I didn't care; I was happy. I knew I would never become a flight attendant, and the only solution I found to have a better life was getting married at 15.

I didn't know what marriage was and the responsibilities that came with it. I thought of escaping home multiple times, but I would break my dad's heart. He loved my siblings and me but didn't know how to show it.

He knew the world was a toxic and dangerous place, especially for women, and he let the fear of losing us to a cruel world take over him. I love him so much, and I forgive him for every trauma I have had in my childhood.

It's not his fault; that's how he was raised and taught to love and protect. As the years passed, your grandfather became softer and softer.

He loved all his grandchildren unconditionally, and you had built amazing memories with him. He changed a lot. He became more caring and talkative, gave advice, and prayed five times daily.

With time, he learned how to show love to his kids and grandkids. Now, he runs to hug us, has coffee with us, looks after us in Lebanon even when we are living in miserable conditions, and doesn't leave us alone.

He helped us take care of his mother. I just wished I had seen this soft part of him when he was younger, not only after he got old. As I said, this was how his parents taught him how to love.

He was trying to protect us from the world's harm. He could have handled it differently. Yes, but back then, I didn't know what he was going through or what he went through in his childhood to make him that way.

My love for him was ever less, even in the harsh days, and my love for him keeps growing more and more. Time passed; I got married, got pregnant, and already had a family when I was 16, and the dream of becoming a flight attendant got buried.

Sometimes, I think about it. Sometimes, I think about what I could have done differently and how my life would have been if I had taken a different path and been stronger if I had dared to run away and start my own life.

It sometimes hurts when I remember how I buried this dream and didn't fight for it, but this was the life God had written for me, and despite everything, I'm grateful.

CHAPTER 8

The Stray Cat

القطة الضالة

My mom gave up on her flight attendant dream, but I didn't. The more I googled about it, the more I fell in love, the more I dreamed, and the more I wanted that life. I would go to all the airline companies' websites to read their requirements and check their flight attendant uniforms and benefits, but no company would beat Dubai Airways. They would promote the dream life my soul was craving for. The only problem is that I was too young to apply for the company. I was 18 years old back then, and the minimum age was 21, so in the meantime, I decided to focus on myself, study the interviews, read every flight attendant blog, learn about the company, and practice my English. I had 3 years to become what they were looking for.

I didn't tell my mom about the dream growing in me daily. I made her believe that I buried it the same way she did with hers. I wasn't scared about her thoughts or reactions; I would rather not disappoint her. I know that, like all the other Arab moms, she would like to see me married and building my own family, even though this was her dream in the past. I wasn't sure how she would digest the news, but I was so excited about the subject that I had to discuss it with someone; I needed an outside opinion, a different perspective, so I decided to share it with Walid and Hamza. They were both in the bedroom playing online games on the computer when I broke the news. I only entered the room and said with a happy smile, "I WANT TO BECOME A FLIGHT ATTENDANT."

They both looked at me with their eyes wide open. Walid smiled and said, "I support you; I want free tickets."

Hamza said with a sarcastic voice and a wide smile and said, "Wow, Baba is going to kill you."

I sat on the bed before them and told them I needed to talk about this. It was killing me every day, keeping it for myself. I told Walid I hadn't slept since he showed me the Dubai videos and introduced me to the Dubai Airways flight attendants. All I could think about was the travels, the lifestyle, and the airplanes, but the thought of having to wait so long for this to become a reality was driving me insane.

"Why don't you start working for local Brazilian airlines first? It will be good for your CV, you will get experience, and it will be easy to join a big airline company like Dubai Airways." Said Walid to me.

I looked at him with my face full of question marks and asked, "What's a CV?"

"Walid covered his face with both his hands and started to scream, 'Oh my God, oh my God!'"

Hamza started to laugh, and he fell on the floor.

Walid had this unbelievable face and asked me if I had lived in Narnia land all this time. After Walid's frustration was over and Hamza stopped laughing, they explained what a CV was. A page with my personal information, a professional photo, work experiences, and schooling background. We went online, and they showed me many CV templates and styles I could create. Thereafter, we started to Google the requirements for the local airlines in Brazil, and they were to have completed high school, be a minimum of 18 years old, and speak Portuguese and Spanish; other languages would be considered a plus. To be medically Fit, To have the ANAC license.

Walid explained to me that ANAC is the national aviation agency of Brazil, and to become a flight attendant, I had to attend a flight attendant course; after completing the course successfully, the ANAC exam should be done and passed with a score higher than 80%. Once passed, I get a flying license where I would be allowed to perform flight attendant duties inside of Brazil for any airline. Thereafter, my brother and I started to Google the flight attendant schools in São Paulo, and we figured out that the courses cost more than a thousand dollars; without the books, uniform, and medical exams, there was a day called survival in the jungle that had to be paid as well. In total, it would cost me money that I didn't have; I was sure my dad wouldn't cover the course price for me and would kill me before I attended the classes. I had no money; Walid and Baba would give me some for my expenses.

"Why don't you take some sealed perfumes from Baba's store and sell them to other stores for a cheaper price? He will not notice if you take one or two per month; it's a good business." Of course, this was Hamza's suggestion.

"Or, you can just find a normal job, like everybody does. Without having to steal your father and pay for your course with your money and hard work." Said Walid, referring to it but looking at Hamza angrily while saying it.

I entirely agreed with him, with Walid, but never with Hamza. This was another challenge I needed to face—to tell my mom and dad I wanted to find a job and be financially independent. I was already smelling the drama. Walid said he would assist me in building a CV or a mini one because I had zero experience and never had a real job; my only job was in Lebanon, supervising the donations during the 2006 war. My advantage was the four languages I spoke, and having lived in different countries like Lebanon and Colombia would make my CV slightly better.

I called my aunt Fatima, and I told her I was searching for a job but that I feared, in case I called for an interview, walking the streets of São Paulo by myself. I had never gone out by myself; it was a big city, and I was always accompanied by a member of my family, who guided us every time we went somewhere.

"Did you tell your parents about you wanting a job? Did they agree to that?" It was the first thing she asked when I told her about my plans. I told her the truth: I had only spoken about this to my brothers and her and would only share it with my parents once I got a job. There was no need for headaches and unnecessary drama ahead of time. I didn't know what my parent's reaction to it would be. I didn't know if they would take it the cool way or if they would say, "A daughter of mine will not work in a foreign country." This story could go sideways. She agreed to take me to the interviews in secret. We would say we were going out to explore the city when, in reality, we would be on the hunt for my first job ever.

Every morning, I would scroll through online job postings, circle newspaper ads, and ask around for connections, hoping to find a position that would help me save money for my flight attendant course. I sent hundreds of CVs to every job vacancy before me, desperate for anything. Hotels, restaurants, clothing companies, airports. I started getting many calls for interviews, and I was saying yes to them. I didn't have any clothes for interviews, either. I had no money to shop for something decent, so I ran to my mom's closet and borrowed her black pants, a white long-sleeve shirt, and black heels.

Aunt Fatima took me to all the interviews; she would wake up early in the morning to go with me; we'd step into the hectic São Paulo streets, take buses, take the full metro, and guide me through the messy streets of São Paulo. I don't think I could arrive at any place by myself; she was a true angel. I did around 13 interviews in different places, but unfortunately, my shitty Portuguese and my foreign background were not helping. Each interview ended with the same reply: "We will let you know; thank you."

After weeks, I would get rejection after rejection, but I didn't let it break me. I had the full support of my aunt. She said, "This is happening because there's something better coming; you just have to trust the process."

She always gave me the motivation never to give up. The more doors slammed in my face, the more determined I became. After a few days, I got a call for another interview, but this time, Auntie Fatima couldn't come with me; she apologized. She had a horrible flu due to the weather change; I told her not to worry, as I wasn't sure if I was going. I didn't pay attention to what the company was about; I only wrote down the address. I woke up the next morning with a mixed feeling; something inside of me was telling me to go, but at the same time, I feared going by myself. I wasn't yet confident to walk alone in the streets of São Paulo. I spent more than half an hour in bed fighting my demons. My mom was still sleeping, my dad and Walid were at work, and Hamza was at school; I decided to stand up and face it. I got dressed, always in the same clothes for all the interviews because it was the only one I had. I made simple makeup, straightened my hair, and left to catch the bus to the metro station.

On that day, everything seemed to go wrong. I got lost inside the metro station; I made multiple wrong stops, and when I finally exited at the right station, I still had to walk for 10 minutes to reach the interview place, and it started to rain. I didn't have any umbrellas with me. It was raining heavily, but I managed to reach the correct location. It was a law firm, and I was late, soaked from head to toe, standing in their shiny marble lobby with my rain-frazzled hair. Even though I was late, they still agreed to interview me. They took me to a room with girls wearing blazers and looking important. They had perfect hair, flawless makeup, and a professional posture that I forgot at home. I felt like a stray wet cat in a room full of expensive Persian cats.

The recruiters brought a Portuguese grammar test, and my stomach twisted. I barely knew how to write properly in Portuguese, I thought. Then, I called the interviewer and explained to her that my Portuguese was weak and that I might be unable to complete that test. She told me that it was okay and that I should try my best, and I did; I did everything I could, scribbling answers and hoping that my effort would count. Then they handed me an English test, and I was so relieved. Of course, I aced the English test. I was leaving that wonderful law firm, where the lobby was all glass, the reception was made of marble, and it smelled like flowers, but as I left, I was sure that I wouldn't hear back from them; it was going to be another rejection e-mail, but I was getting used to it.

"Sorry, do you mind if I ask where your name is from?" one of the receptionists who worked there said.

I replied, "It's originally Persian, but it's a very common name in the Middle East; it means wild rose."

"It's beautiful and different. My name is Kelsey; it's nice to meet you. I hope you get the job. Good luck," she added.

"Thank you. I want it, but I don't think it will happen. There were many perfect candidates, and I showed up like a stray wet cat," I told her, looking disappointed with myself.

"Yes, but none of them has a name that means wild rose," she said with a beautiful smile.

For days, I braced myself for another rejection. I almost didn't pick up when my phone rang, convinced it was bad news. To my shock, it was a call from the interviewer inviting me for a second interview, but this time with the manager. She gently suggested, "This time, try to come with neat hair and a bit of makeup on your face."

Well, I couldn't blame her for warning me how to dress up for an interview after the horror show she had witnessed me in a few days back. The next morning, I woke up 2 hours before the interview time. Full of hope, this was more than most places had given me, so I gathered every ounce of confidence, fixed my hair into a ponytail, applied simple and clear makeup, and arrived 15 minutes earlier at the law firm for my second interview.

This time, it was a more private interview. I was taken to a meeting room and was asked to wait for the manager there. In a room where the table was made of marble and the chairs were pure leather, a waiter came in, gave me a glass of water, placed some cheese bread on the table, and asked me if I would like tea or coffee. I was so ashamed that I only said, "Thank you." I have never had this kind of treatment. I was a village girl who had only been to a shopping mall when she was almost 18, had never seen anything, and was now served like a queen.

The manager entered the room and introduced herself. She said she was impressed with the many languages I speak and the countries I have lived in. She understood that I had weak Portuguese, but she was happy I had good English because they had many international clients, and they needed someone with my English level. She also looked at my CV, asked about my background, and then leaned forward to ask with a calm but curious voice, "Where do you see yourself in five years?"

I stopped for a second to take a deep breath, and part of me hesitated to tell her about my dream of becoming a flight attendant. Maybe that's not what she wants to hear. Maybe that would make it seem like I wasn't committed to the job, but something told me to be myself, and I did. "In five years, I see myself in the skies. I want to be a flight attendant, preferably for Dubai Airways, and hopefully be back in the Middle East, where I can use my languages and culture as an advantage."

Her expression changed, and I could see a soft smile at the corner of her mouth.

"I'm proud of your vision for the future. You know, many of the girls who work here at the reception are ex-flight attendants; that's what we look for, people who have that flight attendant mentality, classy, hospitable, and ready for anything."

I felt a wave of relief. She understood me and said what I had been craving to hear: "You are hired; you got the job."

After she said that, a tear fell from my eyes. I quickly apologized for looking weak before her and cleared that tear. I explained to her that it was a tear of joy; this was my first job and a very important step. She completely understood and gave me a tissue. She said there was no need for me to apologize for being happy. She welcomed me into the team; we shook hands, and I was ready to leave with a mission achieved.

My world was so pink at that moment. After countless rejections, someone finally believed in me and my potential. On my way out, I saw Kelsey in the reception, and I gave her the news; she left her spot and came to hug me, welcomed me into the team, and said she would ask the management for her to be my "godmother," someone they assign to take care of the new receptionist and give all the training needed. As soon as I left the building, I called Aunt Fatima to share the news. Her excitement burst through the phone, and she reminded me that no one can take away what's been written to be mine.

I felt so glad for all the other rejections. None of the companies looked like that fancy law firm, and none of them offered me the benefits they had. I was offered premium medical insurance that would cover absolutely everything, even mental health doctors. A lunch allowance, supermarket allowance. They would pay 50% of my university if I wanted to graduate, and my salary was very high compared to all the other places I went for interviews. Aunt Fatima was right when she said all the rejections were meant to happen because something greater was coming.

CHAPTER 9

The Arabic Girl

البنت العربية

Dinner time at our house was usually calm. Around 7 pm, Walid and Baba would return from their work, and Mama would always prepare the table with Lebanese food. However, that night, I was on the verge of creating a stir with the news that I had secured a job. I wasn't sure about how my parents would react. My father was seated at the head of the table as usual, my mom was opposite him, and Hamza and Walid were next to me. Everyone was eating so peacefully until I cleared my throat and spilled the tea straight away, saying, "I found a job at Paulista Avenue in a very respectable law firm, and I start next week."

My father put the fork down, and my mother, who can sometimes be stricter than him, also paused, looking at me with a shocked face. Walid had his eyes wide open, waiting for what would happen next, and Hamza was moving his shoulders as if he was dancing while seated, waiting for the drama to start. My parents were looking at me, and my father's eye was fixed on me. His face was serious, and he asked, "Who put the idea of working in your head?"

Walid was still staring at me with his eyes open, and I could hear his thoughts saying, "Don't you dare mention my name in this."

I told him no one put anything in my head; I decided this myself. I'm tired of staying home and helping Mom with the cleaning and food. I want to work, have my money, and buy my things. I also told him that things at home were not the greatest and that working would greatly help with the bills. "And who took you to those interviews?" He asked with a strict voice.

I was reluctant to reveal that Aunt Fatima had brought me there, as it could spark a significant argument within the family and jeopardize her reputation as my accomplice. Aunt Fatima was always open-minded; she never liked to follow any cultural rules and always lived life the way she thought was right for her, and I always respected that. She never feared people or their opinions about her. She was that cool aunt who would feed a child ice cream in the morning without his parents knowing. I told my father that I went by myself. I learned how to take buses and the metro, and everything went fine. He kept thinking, staring at me without saying a word, until he took a deep breath and said

"Okay, you want to work, fine! But there will be rules. You can go to work but come straight home when you finish. You are not allowed to get too involved with the Brazilians, go into bars after work, go to parties, or arrive home late. I trust you, Nesrin, and I hope you don't break this trust. We still have our customs in this house, and I don't want you to lose them."

I promised him that I wouldn't disappoint him and that all the customs, traditions, and beliefs would be followed like always. I was so relieved; I wanted to jump from happiness because that was the first step to my biggest dream. My mom didn't say a word at the table. She just nodded to everything my dad said. I was sure that if I screwed this up or did something to upset them, they would take me out of work for good, but I was ready to play by their rules if that was what it took to reach my dreams.

The first day of work at Meester and Werneck law firm had arrived. Of course, I woke up with dragons in my stomach, not butterflies. I wondered if I would fit in there, if they would like me, and how it would be. When I arrived at the law firm, I felt like I had fallen into a world I didn't belong to, a kingdom full of pretty people in suits. It was a giant company, and the whole building, which had 14 floors, belonged to them. As soon as the elevator on the 8th floor opened, I saw the girls waiting for me with their warm smiles and welcoming faces. There were nine of them in total, and each seemed so pretty, confident, elegant, and fancy. I introduced myself, pronouncing my name slowly so they would understand, but it didn't help.

"Don't worry," one of them said, laughing. "We have been practicing your name all morning, but none of us could get it right, so we decided to call you the Arabic girl."

They laughed, and I forced a smile; it wasn't the kind of nickname I expected, but I wouldn't argue on my first day at work. As the day went on, I started to get to know the women who would become my team.

Sara is the most elegant among them. With her perfect nails, her flowery perfume that you could smell throughout the reception, and her perfectly straight hair, I couldn't find a single baby hair out of place. She told me she was a former Japan Airlines flight attendant. She worked there for years until the company broke down and started firing people.

Kelsey is the sweet girl I knew from the interview day. She was assigned to be my godmother and guide me in the job. She told me I was put on two months' probation and that I would do my best work to be fully hired by the company after the two months. We had something in common: we both dreamed of becoming flight attendants. She had completed the ANAC exam course and was still trying to work with the aviation companies.

Paulina was so chilled, had a Zen energy, and always drank green tea. When she told me that before the law firm, she was a flight attendant for Dubai Airways and used to live in Dubai, I went nuts. She worked until first class and then quit the job because she really missed her family back in Brazil.

Tamara seemed to be the sweetest girl, very friendly and approachable. She had this perfect blond hair and a beautiful nose resembling a Barbie. She was also an ex-flight attendant for a Brazilian national airline, Tam, and she was terminated when the company went through a crisis and started to lay off some of its employees. I asked her if she had any Arabic background because Tamara was very popular in the Middle East; she said that her grandfather was Lebanese but didn't relate to Arabs. She considered herself a pure Brazilian.

Thalia, that girl, was a mystery. She was quiet, skinny, had short hair, and was always in her world. I tried to ask a few questions to get to know her better, but she would always change the subject when she didn't want to answer. No one there knew anything about her personal life. All her conversations were professional and about the job.

Hanna was a badass. If confidence had a name, it would be called Hanna. She was tall, had a beautiful posture, and yet was intimidating. She was very honest and would tell you anything directly. She had been in the law firm for years, and she knew everything and everyone. You wouldn't mess with her; she would put you in your place just with one look.

Katrina was the influencer. She was always getting distracted by the fashion news and forgetting to do her tasks. She dreamed of becoming an actress or a model and always followed all the fashionista blogs. Whatever you need to know about fashion and trends, she will give you the best advice.

Mariana was the most sensitive among all the girls. She was very smart and very professional, and at the same time, she was like a fragile orchid petal. I would describe her as the girl from the Power Puff Girls, the blue one (bubbles)

Nanda was the group's clown. She was always making everybody laugh. She had given nicknames to all the lawyers, and the Arabic girl was her idea, too. She had beautiful tan skin, curly hair, and a long mouth that always smiled. I guess she was the one who would bring life to the team.

I already knew the whole team. I wanted to stay longer and talk more with them, especially the ex-flight attendants, to gather some more information about the job, but I couldn't. Kelsey had to take me on a tour around the company.

We started with the meeting rooms, where the lawyers meet with their wallet-loaded clients. Two floors of rooms all looked quite the same, some with bigger tables, all made of shiny marble, and the chairs covered in soft leather. The reception areas on every floor looked just as fancy. The desks were made of marble, and behind each reception was a huge mirror that made the space look bigger and classy, with big pots of fresh orchid flowers on top of the counters that were changed regularly. She showed me the IT room, where people worked quietly with computers and wires, and the copy room, where machines were printing contracts nonstop.

"This is going to be your escape room." She took me to a floor that was just for employees. It had a restaurant where we could buy food, a fridge full of soft drinks and water, shelves with snacks, tea, coffee, and table games, even sofas to lie down and rest, and a room for the employees with a shower and lockers to keep our belongings safe.

She took me back to the reception and explained how the computer works. She taught me how to create meeting reservations, and then she started with the Do's and Don'ts. "Never argue with any lawyer; sometimes they are rude, so you must swallow and move on. You must start memorizing what each lawyer likes to drink and how they like the meeting room to be adjusted. There's a huge mirror behind you, so be careful what you read on the computer so everyone can see. Eating in the reception is not allowed, only drinking tea and water. Everything must be documented, whatever you do. Remember to follow all the rules and never create them yourself. You must also memorize all the lawyer's and their secretaries' names."

It was too much information to absorb, and I tried my best to write it all down. I was overwhelmed and lost with the information and things I had to memorize, but I had to give my best. This was the key to reaching my dreams.

The ensuing two-month probationary period was a complete disaster. I got lost right away. My largest obstacle was the language barrier; my Portuguese was inadequate to keep up, and I could not understand the vocabulary. I had a terrible time writing emails since I didn't know how to utilize the right phrases or format. I was constantly making mistakes and causing trouble. I confused and irritated clients and lawyers by sending them to the incorrect meeting spaces and overlapping reservations. I frequently forgot the lawyers' names and would send them the wrong drink. I frequently forgot to change into heels so that I could bring important and high-class clients to the meeting room in Crocs. My makeup appeared hurried on certain days, and my hair was untidy. The older females had trouble understanding me but always attempted to help. I hadn't adjusted to this new culture, and my attitude was still based on Arabic customs. In little time at all, everyone began to lose it over me. Nobody wanted to work on the same floor as me at one point, and they didn't want to share a reception with me since I always appeared to get into problems. I occasionally stayed late to correct my daytime errors, such as sending incorrect emails, making overlapping reservations, or making incorrect restaurant reservations.

One day, coming back from my lunch break, I overheard some of the girls talking about me, "She's not qualified, she doesn't speak proper Portuguese, and I want to bury my face somewhere every time I read the emails she sends as if she's in high school," said Sara. "This vacancy should have been filled by someone who knows the job," said Hanna

But Tamara commented worse: "I don't know how she wants to be a flight attendant; she cannot do a simple task on the ground, so imagine in the air."

Her words cut deep. I went home that night thinking about everything I heard; deep down, I knew they were right. I was a disaster; I didn't deserve to be employed there. I left that office sad, with tears in my eyes, crying in the metro station while everybody was looking at me. The next morning would be my last probation day, and I knew I wouldn't make it. I went to work with the mentality of "I'm going to miss this place and all the mess I have caused." At the same time, I wouldn't understand why God would place me in a job where most of the girls were ex-flight attendants. I thought it was a sign from the universe. I thought I was destined to be there, but I was wrong.

It was a very tense day; a lawyer stormed into the reception with our manager, furious about a very important document he hadn't received. At the time, Nanda, Hanna, and Mariana were at the desk, and they were the ones responsible for the delivery of the document. I was standing behind the lawyer, listening to all the confrontations. The manager demanded to know what happened to the document, and the lawyer's frustration grew. The girls looked nervous, unsure of how to explain the mistake. Without thinking, I stepped forward. "I'm sorry; it was my fault," I said, my voice trembling and my heart racing, and I continued my speech.

"I'm new to the company, and Portuguese is not my first language. I must have misplaced the document. I didn't understand that I was supposed to send it to you, and I was too ashamed to ask or clarify the information. I'm sorry. This won't happen again."

The lawyer murmured something under his breath and walked away, followed by the manager. As soon as they were gone, the girls turned to me.

"Why did you do that?" Said Hanna.

"Yes, you didn't have to take the blame," said Nanda with a disbelieving face.

"Listen, guys, I know I'm not passing my probation. I have given you a hard time these past two months of probation, and you have done your best and had patience with me, but I'm just being slow to learn and to fit in. I know I'm leaving, and that's fine. I can leave and take this blame with me; I have nothing to lose. I'm new here and still figuring out life in Brazil. You have bills and a family to support, and I won't let you lose this job or get a warning."

They didn't say anything now, but I could see the mix of emotions in their eyes. Even if I was a disaster, I could at least leave knowing I had done something good for someone. After lunch, my manager called me into her office for the probation meeting, which I knew I wouldn't pass. I prepared myself as soon as I sat down and started talking first. - "Thank you so much for everything you have taught me. This was a new world, full of new experiences, and I have learned so much. I understand I don't meet the standards and professionalism you sought. I want you to know I will leave this firm with a grateful heart and a soul at peace."

The manager smiled at me and said, "You have got this all wrong and are staying."

I stared at her, stunned, not understanding anything, and she continued, "The girls came to my office earlier and told me what happened with the document. They admitted it was their fault and said they want you on the team. They feel they haven't given you the training you need and promised to focus on helping you. You are officially hired."

I could hardly believe it. I returned to the reception and found all the girls waiting for me.

"We know what you did, and this was really brave of you; we like perfection, but we also like a good heart, so we like you," said Mariana to me in front of all the girls. They hugged me; I cried and thanked them repeatedly for the second opportunity. From that moment, everything had changed. Nanda taught me how to write emails professionally. Hanna printed pictures of the lawyers she took from the internet, cut them, and made me a journal with their pictures and names next to it. Mariana wrote the preferred drink of each lawyer next to their names and pictures. Kelsey, my godmother, was training me in Portuguese grammar and teaching me new office terminologies. Katrina was teaching me how to fix my hair properly, and she asked me to get rid of the hair bands because not everything that's a trend in Lebanon is also a trend in Brazil.

Thalia helped me with the reservations and gave me tricks on how to avoid getting lost and overlapping meetings. Sara taught me all about etiquette and posture. Paulina taught me how to keep everything under control and not freak out. Tamara apologized to me for not being able to help me much because she was emotionally unavailable and needed to save her energy for an airline interview that was coming soon.

I did learn everything in weeks. I was an entirely new individual, with no delays or overlaps; I maintained control over the floor I was on; I learned how to manage multiple tasks simultaneously; I would place the lawyers' preferred drinks on their table before they entered the room; I would address each one by name; and I would print and present all their documents before they requested them. I was always ahead of them with zero complaints, only compliments. My nickname was still the Arabic girl; some people would call me by my real name, but with a funny spelling. I met a lot of employees who became like family. It was a brand-new word that I finally learned how to fit in.

CHAPTER 10

Building wings

بناء الجناح

It was early morning, and my father was sitting at the kitchen table with his usual ginger tea and lemon, and my mother was sitting next to him, smoking her cigarette like always. I walked down the stairs slowly, my heart pounding; I was so nervous I could barely breathe. I had thought about this moment for weeks, trying to figure out the right words to say, but when the moment came, everything felt harder. Imagine breaking the news to your parents about wanting to become something your community sees with bad eyes. I was never allowed to travel by myself, and if I did, I would only go to places where I had family members, and they would be waiting for me at the airport. Baba would have never let me go to Paris alone to spend my vacation because where I come from, girls are not allowed to travel by themselves.

Now imagine telling him I would want to travel the world without any family member for a living. When I reached the kitchen, I pulled out a chair, looked at them, and then, trembling, started to speak, "Baba, I have something to tell you that is very important for my future." He put down his mug and said, "Here we go, what now? " I have a dream and haven't been able to sleep. It's something I think about every day, every night, every second, and it has been eating me alive. I dream of becoming a flight attendant; I have been saving money to enroll in an aviation school to study aviation."

He stared at me for a moment, and I couldn't tell what he was thinking. Was he going to slap me in the face? Tell me to go back to my room and stop saying nonsensical things. Or was he going to kick me out of the house? My mom's face looked at me as if she was having déjà vu. I was the younger version of her, fighting for what she didn't dare to fight.

"This job is too risky; it's not the career I want to see you pursue. We expect you to get married, find a man who will treat you right, build a family, and if you want to work, then find a respectable job, but this. What are people going to say about my daughter traveling the world? Serving alcohol inside an airplane? Sleeping in hotels by herself? They will say we didn't know how to raise you and that you are a lost girl."

I felt my heart sink, but I tried to remain calm and not have a mental breakdown in front of him. My mom finally said it was just a course; it meant nothing. She told him to let me study and that there was no harm in studying and getting more knowledge. We went back and forth discussing this crazy dream of mine; he even got late to work because of me. I tried too hard to convince him with the support of my mom. I told him how hard I had worked to save money and explained how important this step was for me. Until he finally agreed to go for the course, but not work as a flight attendant, only studying.

This was already an important step in my career; with time, I would convince him slowly about the profession and make him see that there is nothing shameful about being a flight attendant. I couldn't contain my excitement; I stood up and hugged and kissed him repeatedly, thanking him for allowing it to happen. I felt an overwhelming sense of relief and gratitude. It wasn't just permission; it was the start of my dream coming to life.

That same day, I left home early because I needed to go to the aviation school to start my registration. I walked into the school with a mixed feeling; I was excited and nervous at the same time. Of course, as always, nobody could pronounce my name correctly. It had become a familiar challenge and part of my routine to arrive somewhere, spell my name, and explain where it originated. After paying all the fees, I was officially enrolled. My life became like an airplane passing through turbulence for the next few months. Every morning, I would leave home at 7 am, go to the aviation school, and after classes, I would go straight to work. My days were long. I wouldn't return home until 11 pm each night, exhausted but motivated, and my dad would be there by the door waiting for me to arrive every night.

At the aviation school, I was thrown into a whole new universe. There was so much to learn, like aviation maintenance, the history of aviation, the hijackings, tragedies, and even the terrorist attacks. Everything was taught in Portuguese, which added an extra layer of challenge, but I pushed through. Beyond the technical knowledge, we were also trained in etiquette and presentation. I learned to make soft and neat makeup like a flight attendant and present myself with poise and confidence. The training was intense, and they also prepared us for every possible scenario we might face in the skies.

One of the most memorable experiences was called "Survival in the Jungle." They took us into the wilderness for a full day, where we had to survive independently. It was both terrifying and thrilling. We also practiced evacuating from a smoke-filled room and finding our way despite the chaos. In another scenario, we were made to jump into a freezing pool, simulating an emergency water landing. The cold was shocking, but it taught us to stay calm and act quickly under pressure. The course wasn't just about serving passengers, asking for chicken or beef. And keep smiling at the passengers; it was about preparing us for the worst and being ready for anything. It was strict, rigorous, full of rules to be followed, exhausting, and expensive, but every moment felt worth it.

I made friends during the course, though fitting in wasn't always easy. Most of my colleagues were wild and full of dreams, living very different lives from mine and having the freedom my soul always craved. But we all had one thing in common: the dream of becoming a flight attendant. Everyone studied hard, fighting to pass the exams and prove we were ready for the skies. Eventually, the course ended, and we faced our final exam; it was nerve-wracking, but I passed.

The final exams were done, and the end of the aviation course was near. One day, the school made an exciting announcement: a highly respected Brazilian airline was recruiting flight attendants and coming to our school to interview students for the role. This was the opportunity I had been waiting for, and without hesitation, I subscribed to attend the interview scheduled for two days later at 5 pm., but there was a problem; I had to work during that time. I asked Hanna if she would change the timings with me. I would take her morning shift, and she would take my day shift for one day. I explained the reason, and she immediately agreed, saying she wanted to see me shining in the skies. We asked the approval from our manager to trade the timings, and to my relief, she agreed.

The interview day had arrived, and I went in early to work on Hanna's place. I was working on the same floor as Tamara, one of my coworkers who has become a friend. It was a very busy time, full of meetings and many special requests from lawyers; when we finally had some time to breathe, I told Tamara about the local airline being at the aviation school today to recruit new flight attendants. She seemed very positive and supported me in my decision. She also took a flight attendant course and worked for a local airline. She said it would be a good experience and that it is hard to find someone who speaks Arabic in the aviation field in Brazil. Her encouragement gave me hope. As the clock ticked closer to my interview time, I asked Tamara if she was okay with me leaving the reception 10 minutes earlier to go down and change my clothes for the interview, and she agreed.

I gathered all my things—keys, papers to practice more for the interview, and aviation school ID—and threw everything inside my bag. I ran quickly to the toilet on the same floor, returned, grabbed my bag, got a good luck kiss and hug from Tamara, and went downstairs to change. When I arrived, the entrance was crowded with students, all eager for their chance. At the door, they asked me for my school ID. I reached into my bag to grab it, but it wasn't there. I searched again, emptying all the items in my bag onto the counter, but the ID was nowhere to be found. I started to panic; I begged the lady to let me in, not to let me lose the chance; she knew I was a student there. She wouldn't agree and called the school principal.

And I begged the school principal to let me in, but she said, "I know who you are, and I know you study here. You are the only Arabic student here with a different name, but if you can't follow the standards on your interview day, imagine after you become a flight attendant. No airplane will delay its takeoff until you get your hands on your ID; it's the same here."

Her words hurt, but I couldn't argue. I stood there helpless as the opportunity slipped from my fingers. I left the school in tears, devastated.

The next morning, I went to work feeling completely drained. My heart was heavy, and every step I took felt like a reminder of what I had lost. The dream I worked so hard on felt farther away than ever. When I arrived at the reception, I found Tamara, Hanna, and Mariana chatting. Hanna immediately noticed me and said excitedly and loudly, "How was the interview?"

I told her straight away that there was no interview. The three girls looked at me with their shocked faces. I sat down, and I explained to them everything that had happened to me. Mariana jumped immediately and said, "That doesn't make any sense. If it had fallen here, someone would have found it. We all know your name, and anyone who found it would have returned it to the reception. What would they do with an aviation ID? Nothing. It would have been returned already."

Her logic made sense, but I still couldn't figure out what had happened; Hanna joined the conversation and said, "Let's think this through. When exactly did you last see the ID?"

I remember sitting here. It was a very busy day. I decided to leave 10 min-utes earlier. I grabbed everything, including the ID, and threw everything inside the bag. I left it in the reception. I went to the toilet to pee, returned, grabbed my bag, and went downstairs to change.

Hanna's eyes lit up, and she came up with an idea; she suggested we speak to the management to get the footage from the security camera to understand what must have happened to that ID and if I lost it inside the office. Before I could respond to her idea, Tamara jumped in and said, "That's ridiculous; management isn't going to waste time going through security footage for a lost school ID. It had nothing to do with the job and did not endanger the firm's security. It's just a waste of time, and they will never agree."

Her reaction felt weird, but I agreed, trying to avoid making things worse and turning this ID into a Mexican telenovela. I told them Tamara was right; the company wouldn't take that seriously. I suggested we forget about the whole thing; it wasn't worth it. Even if I did find that ID, nothing was going to change. I had lost my shot at building my wings, and I couldn't shake the weight of guilt from my shoulders. It was a very irresponsible move that prevented me from reaching my dreams. There was no going back. No fixing it. All I had to do was accept and move on.

CHAPTER 11

Broken Wings

أجنحة مكسورة

A year and a half had passed since I finished the aviation course, and my dream of becoming a flight attendant felt further away than ever. None of the airlines in Brazil were hiring, and the only opportunities were with international airlines. But there was one catch: I needed to be at least 21 years old to apply. Still working at the law firm, my days were routine but unfulfilling. While working on the same floor as Paulina and Tamara, one day, Paulina brought news that made my heart beat. "Dubai Airways is coming to São Paulo to recruit cabin crew; have you heard about it?

I froze when I listened to what she said. I told her that's my dream airline to work for, but I can't apply because I'm not 21 yet.

"You can still apply even if you haven't reached 21 yet, silly! Go to the interview. If you pass, they'll hire you but only take you to Dubai once you turn 21."

Those words came out of Paulina's mouth and restored my hope. She made it sound so simple, so possible. I was 20 and a half, so why not? My heart was full of hope. "I'll do it," I said, determination rising in my chest. Paulina then mentioned that Tamara was also planning to go, so we agreed to attend together. Paulina explained the process to me in detail. The first stage was an open day, which was done by a third party, not Dubai Airways recruiters. I didn't need to register online. I just had to show up at the hotel dressed in business attire with my CV and photos. If I passed the Open Day, I'd receive an email inviting me to Assessment Day, which was more intense with group dynamics, English tests, and scenario-based exercises, and this was done by the professional Dubai Airways recruiters who came straight from Dubai to pick the flight attendants. If all the stages of the assessment day were passed, then I would get another email with another date and an invitation to attend the final interview, which would be around one hour face-to-face with the recruiter.

The Open Day arrived, and I dressed carefully, a skirt, blazer, white shirt, stockings, and simple makeup. Tamara and I entered the hotel, joining a room of around 600 souls, all dreaming of the same job and life in Dubai. The energy was electric, but my nerves were overwhelming. We were split into groups and seated in circles. I had to read a text in English and introduce myself. My voice and hands trembled, and I could feel my breath catching in my throat. I feared looking the recruiter in the eye or looking at any of the candidates. Tamara wasn't in the same circle; she was in another group just behind me.

The process was very fast, and they only did it to test our English and our personalities. The day went fast; we returned home, hoping to hear good news from them. I remember taking the metro and praying to get accepted to the second stage. That same night, Tamara sent me a message saying she had received an unsuccessful email from the recruiting company. I desperately ran to open my email, and there it was, the same email as hers, of my dream being rejected. I didn't even pass the second stage of the interview. I was sad, but I didn't lose hope. At the end of the email, it was written that they would come back to São Paulo in 3 months and that I could re-apply again.

I spent the next three months devouring every cabin crew blog, learning how to present myself better, what to say, and how to act. When Dubai Airways announced another Open Day, I returned wearing the same clothes but carrying a deeper sense of preparation. This time, I felt more confident. But once again, I didn't make it. Neither did Tamara, but this time was different; I didn't have to wait for any email, and the rejection was straight to my face. They said I needed to practice more my English, but my English didn't need practicing. The thing is, when I get nervous, I swallow a few words, and this anxiety of mine kills me alive. This rejection hit me harder the second time, and I felt hopeless. I left that hotel lobby in tears and kept crying until I got home with my eyes swollen. It was a weekend, and I had told my parents I had an extra shift at work; I never told them I had been going to a flight attendant interview.

The moment I entered home with my crying face and swollen eyes, I saw my mom's family in the living room. Uncle Othman and Aunt Lamia were visiting. I said hello to them with hugs and kisses, and I excused myself and went upstairs to wash my face and clean the mascara that was all over my face. Uncle Othman noticed my unusual behavior and came upstairs, knocked on my bedroom door, and asked me if he could come in for a quick chat; he sat down beside me, his expression a mix of concern and curiosity.

"Your parents are worried about you," he began. "You've been acting strange, crying, anxious, avoiding everyone. They think there's a reason behind it." He paused, then leaned closer. "They think you're involved with a Brazilian guy. Is it true?"

I couldn't help but laugh bitterly. Then the dam broke. I told him everything: about the Dubai Airways interviews, the rejections, and how much it hurt.

"I've been dreaming of becoming a flight attendant forever. I worked hard, and I tried my best when the opportunity came. But I was rejected, not once, but twice. I feel like my wings are broken, like I'm falling, and there's no way to fix them."

Uncle Othman listened quietly, letting me pour my heart out, and then he said a quote to me that I had been carrying with me forever, "Don't rush the river; it runs by itself. Maybe what you wanted so much didn't work out, but it doesn't mean it won't last forever; maybe it is just not the right time; you need to have patience and trust God's timing. But for now, you need to talk to your parents. They don't know what's happening, and their imaginations run wild. Come downstairs and explain to them. It's time." I hesitated, but he insisted, and soon I found myself in the living room with my parents, my aunt Lamia, and my uncle Othman.

My dad looked at me expectantly. "What's going on?" he asked. I took a deep breath and began, "It's not what you think. I don't have a Brazilian boyfriend. That's all in your heads." My mom exhaled loudly, clasping her hands together, "Oh, thank God. I could never bear the disgrace." "Mama, you don't need to worry about me that way. I know the rules, the traditions. I know I'm only supposed to marry a Muslim guy. But that's not what's been bothering me." I opened up completely in front of the entire family for the first time.

The truth is, I've been struggling because of my dream. I want to become a flight attendant, and I've worked hard for it. I attended the aviation course. I studied every detail. And then, I had the opportunity to interview for Dubai Airways. I've tried twice, but I was rejected both times. The first time was hard enough, but the second time broke me."

My dad's expression changed in an instant, and for a second, I thought he was going to beat me up like my grandfather did to my mom.

"What? Did you go to those interviews without consulting us? Who permitted you to take such a step? Do you think I would ever allow you to become a flight attendant?" Said Baba, shouting and losing his temper. I heard Aunt Lamia whispering a phrase in Arabic, which meant in English, "Like mother, like daughter."

طب الجرة على تمها بتطلع البنت
لامها

The exact Arabic words sounded heavier, and I gave her a killer look. I wanted to stab the woman. She destroyed my mom's dream in the past, and I wasn't going to allow her to do the same to mine. After I gave her the look of I will murder you, I turned back to my dad and continued by saying with my eyes already filling with tears, "I didn't tell you because I knew you wouldn't support me."

"You cannot make these decisions without talking to us first. Do you know what this job means? What would it look like to others? People would think I didn't raise you properly. They would say I allowed my daughter to take a job that's not respectable." He said to me, screaming and furious.

Of course, Aunt Lamia interfered in our conversation with her sharp tone and spitting poison. This kind of job isn't for you. You're wasting your time. You should be focusing on getting married. Look at your cousins; they're all engaged or married already. And here you are, getting older, unmarried, and giving headaches to your parents, acting like a Westernized person."

I tried to hold back tears as she continued, "And even if your parents allowed you to pursue this madness, do you know how competitive these jobs are? Thousands of girls apply, and they only pick the best, the prettiest, the ones who look like models. You don't have what it takes to compete with them."

Her words stung deeply. I felt exposed and defeated, and my dad agreed with every word she said. "She's right," said my dad. This isn't a job for someone from our background. It's not meant to be. Please, get this idea out of your mind. Think about your future, building a family, and something more stable."

Uncle Othman stepped in to soften the tension; he turned to me and said, "Speaking of the future, I've been thinking about someone for you to meet. His name is Ziad; he's the son of a very good friend of mine. He's a lawyer, Lebanese-Brazilian, Muslim, from a village close to ours in Lebanon, works very hard to get what he wants, and his parents are looking for a bride for him, and I thought of you as a perfect match for him. I gave him your number, and he should contact you soon."

"Tell him she will meet with him, and she will get rid of this idea of traveling the world by herself. If he's a respectful and good man, she can meet him and start getting to know him, " said my dad, still shouting and angry at the whole situation.

The next day, I got a message from Ziad. He introduced himself, saying that my uncle had given him my number and that he wanted to get to know me. We agreed to meet at an ice cream place close to my house. When I arrived, I immediately saw him: a tall guy with a warm smile, a neat beard like most Arab men, and big brown eyes that stood out. He was handsome, no doubt about it, but something felt off. He wasn't what I was looking for. We sat at a small table in the corner on a big blue couch under a huge, messy baby frame, eating an ice cream. At first, the conversation felt forced. I didn't want to be there, and I could tell he didn't either. There were long pauses, and neither of us knew what to say. Finally, I decided to break the tension. I looked at him and said, "Listen, I don't think I'm what you're looking for."

He raised his eyebrows, made a confused face, and asked what I meant by that. "I just want to be honest; I don't want to get married. It's never been in my plans. I don't picture myself in a big white dress at some huge Arabic wedding. I haven't even thought about marriage or kids. All I've ever wanted is to become a flight attendant. That's been my dream for as long as I can remember, but my parents are against it. I don't have their support, and now I'm sitting before you to please them."

He nodded slowly, taking it in. Then he looked at me with a small, sad smile and said, "I appreciate your honesty, so I guess I'll be honest too. I never saw myself marrying an Arab girl. I've been with a Brazilian woman for years. I love her. But my parents, especially my mom, are against this union. They want me to marry a Muslim girl from our culture. My mom even said she'd cut ties with me if I ever decided to marry the love of my life."

For a moment, we sat in silence. His story sounded so much like mine: two people trapped by expectations we didn't ask for, being forced to follow a path we didn't want to make others happy. Then, an idea hit me. I leaned forward, lowering my voice. "What if we made a deal?" He shook his head, curious, and had his eyes wide open, looking at me. He said with a curious voice, "What kind of deal?" "Let's make our parents happy. We'll pretend we're getting to know each other, that we like each other, maybe even fake love each other. And then...we can get married. But it'll be all pretend, like a theater." "A fake marriage?" he asked with a tone of voice a bit more elevated and a surprised face.

"Yes! We'll keep our lives separate. We will be a happy couple for society and our parents, but we will live separate lives and have separate beds. You can continue your love story with your girlfriend, and I'll never interfere. Meanwhile, I can focus on my career. Once we're married, you'll be responsible for me, and if I get a flight attendant job, my parents can't stop me. I'll be free to go because my husband would allow me to. Once I achieve my dream, I will be far away from here, where none of them could reach me or interfere in my life or yours, and you will be a free man to do and be with whoever you want; it's a win-win situation."

He stared at me for a moment, then burst into laughter. "You're joking. Is this some twisted humor of yours, or are you damn for real?" I'm serious; think about it. Your mom will be happy because you'll marry a Muslim girl. My parents will be happy because they think I'm finally settling down. And in the end, we both get what we want." I said, laughing even more, but I meant every word I said. He leaned back in his chair, his expression thoughtful. "You're serious about this?" "Completely," I said.

"You're something else. But okay, I'm in. On one condition: you must promise you'll be committed to this. We must act the part, or it won't work." He said. I extended my hand, meeting his gaze, and promised that the deal would never be broken, at least not from my side. He took my hand and shook it. For the first time that evening, we both felt comfortable with each other. The tension was completely gone. We had a plan that was risky, crazy, dangerous, and unconventional, but it was ours, and we were going to make it work. It was the only way to get the happy ending we deserved. A way of gaining control of our future, writing our own stories with our pen, and gaining authority over the path we choose to follow in life. It was a sacrifice we were both willing to make to be happy finally.

CHAPTER 12

The Angel

الملاك

Months passed, and Ziad and I kept talking. To our parents, it looked like we were getting to know each other for marriage. But in reality, we were just friends, playing along with the plan to keep everyone happy. Whenever I told my parents I would meet Ziad, I wasn't meeting him. I'd go to the bookstore instead, spending hours flipping through books, letting my mind escape into different stories.

Meanwhile, Ziad would tell his parents he was meeting me, but I'd go out with his Brazilian girlfriend instead. He told me that he had explained the whole plan to his girlfriend and that she was okay with it. She accepted it as something he had to do for his family and trusted him. It was strange, but it worked. We kept faking it, pretending until it became second nature. Of course, there were times when we had to meet, like when his family came to visit mine or when my family visited him. Those moments felt like performances. We'd sit together, smiling politely, while our parents watched us with hopeful eyes. Then, they'd leave us alone to "get to know each other." And we did get to know each other, but not as lovers. We talked like friends, opening up about everything: our lives, future plans, work, goals, and dreams. We didn't hold back because there was no pressure between us.

I began to see that Ziad was a really good person. He was polite and kind, always respectful. He had big dreams for his future and worked hard to achieve them. He was smart, ambitious, and driven, which reminded me a lot of myself, but we differed in important ways. We wanted different things in life and love. I wanted to fly and see the world; he wanted stability and a family. We were walking separate paths, but we could share them in those moments, like travelers meeting on the road. Even though we didn't have feelings for each other, there was a connection between us, a kind of understanding that made everything easier.

One day, I arrived at work and immediately felt something strange. The energy in the reception was heavy. Some girls looked happy, smiling and chatting, while others had serious, closed expressions. It felt tense, and I couldn't figure out why. I approached Katrina and asked what was happening because something felt off. She leaned in and whispered, "Some girls got emails about a raise in their salaries, and others didn't."

I went to check my email straight away, but I wasn't one of the girls who got the raise. I wasn't surprised, though. Most girls who received raises were older than me and more experienced. They'd been working there much longer. Still, I couldn't help but feel a little disappointed. It wasn't fair; in my vision, everybody should be treated equally, but what could I do? I walked to the restroom. There, I found Thalia crying. Seeing her like that surprised me. She was always quiet and composed, never showing emotions; the girl was like a robot with human blood. I approached her carefully and asked, "Are you okay? What's wrong?"

Through her tears, she said, "I didn't get the raise. I worked so hard all year, and it's just not fair. I'm just so demotivated. I worked hard the whole year, never called in sick, never got a warning, and was always on time, and this is how they thank me. I have a family to support, and this raise would have made a big difference."

Thalia wasn't someone I was close to. She was the kind of colleague who kept everything private. She knew how to set boundaries and separate work from private life. Nobody at work knew anything about her personal life. She never shared any personal stories, nobody had her as a friend on Facebook or Instagram, and she didn't engage in small talk unless it was about work, and she was right about everything she mentioned. She was incredibly disciplined, always on time, never calling in sick, and prepared for everything. She was one of the best workers we had. I needed to comfort her somehow, so I hugged her and said, "I'm sorry, Thalia. You deserve to be recognized. Just because they didn't give you a raise doesn't mean you're not good enough. Everyone knows how hard you work. You're one of the best among us, and you shouldn't let this bring you down, demotivate you, or even doubt yourself for a second."

I don't know what came over me, but I suddenly had an idea. I looked at her and asked, "Have you ever thought about becoming a flight attendant?" She blinked, surprised, and with her hands full of napkins trying to dry her tears, she said, "What? No, I've never even considered it. I don't think I'd be good at it." "Why not?" I said. "You're disciplined, organized, and hardworking. I'm sorry they didn't see your value here, but maybe it's time to try something different. Flight attendants earn well, and you need the money, right? You can try; it's worth a shot."

I told her about Dubai Airways and how they'd recruit in São Paulo that month. She hesitated, saying she didn't think she had what it took to be a flight attendant. But I reassured her, reminding her of how professional, disciplined, and attentive to details she was, and one of the best among all the girls. Why wouldn't she be just as amazing in the air? Of course, I told her it would be fine if she didn't like the idea; some people hate planes and their lifestyles and can't live without a routine But there was no harm in trying if she was open to it. Thalia hugged me and thanked me for the idea and for listening. She would think about everything and let me know. Later that day, Thalia sat next to me in the reception. She looked calm but serious and said, "I thought about it; I want to try. Can you help me and guide me through the whole process?"

I was surprised but happy. For the first time, I had a conversation with that girl that wasn't office-related. I told her everything I knew: what to wear, what to bring, and how to prepare. I showed her the Dubai Airways website, the blogs I'd read, and the YouTube videos I'd watched. She wrote everything down and said she would read and watch everything until the interview day arrived. She even shared how weird she was feeling about it because it was never something she had thought about, and it never even crossed her mind to apply to become a flight attendant. She even used an expression in Portuguese that they use to describe a feeling: "I feel like walking blindfolded in a shooting field," and I laughed.

I told her there's always something new to learn, discover, and try! I spent the whole week in that office, seeing that girl reading about aviation, Dubai life, and the history of how Dubai Airways started to build their wings, watching and reading flight attendants blogs sharing their flying life, and I was always there answering all her doubts and questions. She had trouble knowing how to get dressed for the interview, and we went shopping together, hunting for the perfect outfit. We would sit together and have lunch every day. She started to open up slowly to me; it was the first time I felt close to her; she was becoming more than a colleague. I always thought she was a little bit weird, but like they say, "Never judge a book by its cover." She was only weird from the outside, but when I got to know her, she was a fighter, a hard worker, full of feelings, sensitive, and she could even be funny sometimes.

When the Open Day arrived, Thalia and I went together. It was my third time applying, so I was less nervous, especially with her by my side. Tamara was there, too, and when she saw Thalia, she made a surprised and shocked face and asked, "What are you doing here?"

Thalia explained to her calmly how I introduced her to the flight attendant word, and she said there was no harm in giving it a shot, as she needed a new job with higher pay so she could keep supporting her family. I stared at Tamara's face. She didn't seem to like the idea of Talita being there, though I didn't understand why she was so bothered by it. The Open Day was like the others I had attended. Always with 600+ people trying to turn their dreams into reality. All were divided into groups like the previous ones, introducing ourselves and answering short questions to test our English and study our personalities. I answered a bit more confidently this time, and so did Talia and Tamara. I crossed my fingers, hoping this time I would move forward.

I got called on the side by one of the interviewers who wasn't part of the Dubai Airways team; he was a third-party company performing the open day on behalf of the aviation company. He told me that my skirt and blazer were a bit tight and that I should try my best to get back fitter the next time. I accepted the feedback positively, and he was correct; I was slightly above my average weight. From the time he gave me that feedback, I was sure I hadn't made it. Something inside me broke completely, and I always tried to keep it together. It would be one more door shut in my face, one more "NO," and I think rejection was starting to be part of my routine. I didn't tell any of the girls about the feedback; I kept the disappointment to myself. Before we left, Thalia made us promise not to tell anyone at work about her attending the interview. She was always private and didn't want anyone to know. I promised her I'd take the secret to the grave, and Tamara agreed. I got home trying to act normal so I wouldn't upset my parents again for not removing that career from my head.

The next day at the office, I got the email and was accepted to the second stage, Assessment Day. For the first time, I'd made it past the first stage. Thalia also received an email, and so did Tamara. The three of us were overjoyed. We jumped and hugged, celebrating our small victory. It felt like a dream was coming closer to reality. For Thalia, it wasn't a lifelong dream, but for me and Tamara, this meant everything. I ran to the office toilet and called Ziad; I didn't know why he was the person I wanted to share this news with. He was genuinely happy for me; he said he would support me until I made it true and was sending positive vibes and prayers for me to do well in the second stage.

It was time to start preparing for Assessment Day, a full day of group dynamics, English tests, and challenging scenarios. It was intense, but I felt a new kind of hope that it would happen the next day. Thalia was panicking because the assessment day would be with the recruiters from Dubai Airways, who would be sent straight from Dubai to pick their best candidates. She was nervous; she didn't know how to do her makeup and hair properly and probably wouldn't be sleeping the whole night practicing how to act in the interview. I offered to sleep at my place, and she agreed straight away, but I made sure she didn't open her mouth to anyone at home about the interview; otherwise, she would attend my funeral and not the interview. I contacted my neighborhood hairdresser; her name was Jill, and she was always there for me every time I needed her. She said she would open the salon at 6 am to fix our hair and make it a French twist like the Dubai Airways flight attendant. Chris, the massage therapist, who was also a makeup artist in the neighborhood, would be there waiting for us to transform us into real flight attendants.

The night Thalia slept at my place, I opened up to her. I told her I was sure I wouldn't pass to the second stage because the interviewer cemented my weight, and the email surprised me. For the first time, she told me about her personal life, where she lived, how many brothers and sisters she had, the countries she visited, and where she learned English. I learned everything about her, and we couldn't sleep, so we spent the whole night talking about ourselves and our good and bad moments.

The morning of the assessment day arrived, and Thalia and I, who barely managed to sleep due to the anxiety and stress of that day, had our makeup perfectly done, our hair was neat, and our outfits were polished. We looked exactly how flight attendants should look: professional, elegant, and ready for the skies. We took the metro to the hotel where the interview was being held. As we entered the hotel lobby, the air felt different from the Open Day. Tamara was already there waiting for us, and we greeted her before looking around. Unlike the Open Day, which had over 600 people, only about 80 were on the assessment day. It felt like such an honor to be among this smaller group. Getting there was already a big accomplishment, and I was proud to have made it that far. The recruiters explained the structure of the day. There would be three stages:

1. A group dynamic exercise.

2. An English test.

3. A final group dynamic exercise.

But there was a catch: you had to pass the first group dynamic before moving on to the English test. You'd be sent home right after the first stage if you didn't pass. We were divided into smaller groups and asked to sit in circles. The task was to talk to the person next to us, learn about them, and then introduce them to everyone else. It sounded simple enough, but my anxiety started building the moment it was my turn. My voice trembled when I stood to introduce the person next to me. My hands shook, and I felt my legs struggling to stay still. The Dubai Airways recruiters walked around the room, watching us closely. They didn't just listen to what we said; they observed everything: our body language, how we spoke, how we carried ourselves. It felt like they were analyzing every detail.

After everyone finished, we sat back down, waiting for the results. The recruiters handed out envelopes. The message would tell us whether we were moving to the next stage. I opened mine slowly, my hands trembling. The words hit me like a punch to the stomach: "We're sorry. Please try again next time. You did not pass to the next stage."

I sat there in silence, staring at the letter. It felt like my heart had sunk to the floor. All my preparation, all my hopes, it was over, just like that. Tamara walked over to me, holding her envelope. Her face was pale, and she looked shocked.

"I didn't pass," she said, her voice shaking. "I can't believe I didn't pass."

I barely had the energy to respond. I just nodded, feeling the heaviness of disappointment pressing down on me. From across the room, I saw Talia waving at me. She was smiling, her face glowing with excitement.

"I made it! I made it! Did you?" She called out.

I couldn't bring myself to say anything. I just moved my head left and right, giving her the "no" signal; she looked at me; her smile faded for a second, but then they called her name to move to the next room. She waved goodbye, and I waved back, forcing a small smile as I silently wished her good luck. As she disappeared into the next room, I sat there, feeling a mix of sadness, pride for her, and frustration with myself. I didn't know what else I could have done better to change the results or my destiny. Leaving the hotel after the interview was one of the hardest walks of my life. My legs felt heavy, and my heart felt even heavier.

The rejection still echoed in my mind. I had tried so hard, and yet it wasn't enough. I told myself I needed to pull it together on the way home. My parents couldn't know where I had been or what had happened. But I've never been good at hiding my emotions, and the tears had already left their mark. My eyes were red, my face was pale, and anyone who looked at me could tell something was wrong. When I got home, I tried to fake it. I walked in, pretending everything was fine but couldn't keep it up for long. My mom immediately noticed and asked me what was wrong with the concern in her voice and the worry in her face. My dad looked at me, too, and asked, "Did something happen?" Even my brothers stopped what they were doing, and their eyes were fixed on me. I answered them with a cold "Nothing," looking down, avoiding eye contact. But my mom wasn't convinced and asked, "Did you fight with Ziad?"

I froze. I didn't know what to say. I couldn't tell them the truth; I would put our plan at risk, and they would stab me on the spot. She came to sit next to me on the sofa and started to give me her love advice with a firm tone of voice: "Listen to me, don't screw this up. Ziad is a good man. Many girls would dream of having someone like him or marrying someone like him. Don't let a fight ruin everything. You need to talk to him and resolve the matter Don't take things too seriously; crying won't solve anything. Tomorrow, meet with him and clear whatever misunderstanding is going on between both of you."

In her mind, my tears and my sadness could only mean one thing: that I had a problem with Ziad. For a second, I was glad she thought that was the problem. Even though I was dressed up, looking like a flight attendant from head to toe, I would always tell them that I was participating in the firm's events on the weekend for extra cash, and they would always believe it. After all the parenting talk, I looked at her, and all I could say was, "I don't want to talk about it." My voice cracked, and I stood before she pressed me further. I went straight to my room, closed the door, and fell onto my bed. I was emotionally exhausted. The rejection, the pressure, the pretending. I just wanted to escape it all. And so, I slept, hoping to feel a little better when I woke up.

I woke up early the next day, Monday morning, to my phone ringing. It was Thalia. Her voice was shaky, almost desperate.

"I passed all the stages of the assessment day! They called me for the final interview, which is today, and I don't know what to do. I called in sick for work because I can't miss it. I need your help. Can you meet me at the metro station before you go to work this afternoon? Could you fix my hair and makeup? I don't know how to do it, and I can't mess this up."

Still groggy, I told her, "Of course I will be there," feeling a mix of pride and sadness. A few hours later, I met her at the metro station's public toilet. When I saw her, we hugged tightly. I congratulated her, trying to put my own feelings aside. "You made it so far, and on your first try! That's an incredible achievement. You should be proud of yourself."

But Thalia didn't look as happy as I expected. She hesitated, then said softly, "I feel like I'm stealing your dream. I feel awful about it. I don't know if I should even go ahead with this."

Her words hit me hard, but I didn't want her to carry this guilt. I took a deep breath and told her, "Don't feel that way. I grew up hearing the same quote repeatedly: What is meant to be yours will find you. Even if there's a mountain between you and what you want. If it's written to be yours, it will be. Nobody can change that. I'm happy for you, Thalia, truly. But I won't lie; I'm sad for myself. Still, I'm here for you. I'll be by your side, cheering for you until you make it to the end."

After that, I got to work. I fixed her makeup, styled her hair, and ensured everything looked perfect. When I was done, I gave her a tight hug. She thanked me, her eyes filled with gratitude, and said to me before she left for her final interview, "You are the angel God sent to my life to guide me."

"Good luck. You've got this." These were my final words to her with a soft smile and a broken heart. It was still too early for me to go to work, and I felt like I couldn't hold in my emotions anymore. So, I called Ziad and asked if he could meet me. When we met, I couldn't stop the tears. Everything I had been holding in—the rejection, the disappointment, the heartbreak—came flooding out. I told him everything that had happened, from the interview to helping Thalia prepare for hers. Ziad didn't say much. He just pulled me into a hug and let me cry. He kissed me on the forehead for the first time, a gesture so unexpected and kind that it broke me even more.

"You don't have to stay here with me," I told him through my tears. You'll be late for work." "Here is exactly where I should be," he said with his soft voice. For the first time in a long time, I felt like someone truly understood my weight.

CHAPTER 13

Romeo And Juliet

رومیو و جولییت

Ziad and I were getting closer every day. We started meeting regularly. We would always meet at our ice cream spot and sit there for hours, swapping playlists. His music taste was entirely different from mine. He loved Brazilian songs, while I couldn't stand them. I was all about Arabic music and its drama; he couldn't stand it. But it was fun to share and laugh about how opposite we were. We would discuss life and our dreams and vent about everything going on in our personal and professional lives.

He became someone I could trust completely. He was always there for me, and I was always there for him as friends, nothing more. I loved spending time with Ziad. He had this way of making everything feel lighter. I could tell him anything, and he'd always listen carefully before giving advice. His words always seemed to soothe my heart or provide a fresh perspective. Even though he was seven years older than me, we connected easily. He had so much life experience and was chatty, warm, and friendly. It was hard not to enjoy his company. One day, he opened up about his girlfriend. "We've been fighting a lot; she's getting jealous and uncomfortable about how often we meet. She doesn't like that we're pretending to be a couple."

I had seen it coming. Jealousy was inevitable in a situation like this. I'm sure she wished she was in my place, loved by his parents, frequenting his house, eating his mom's food, and being able to hug and kiss him in front of the entire family without shame. Playing Xbox with his brothers and planning family trips. It was like she was always his shadow. I used to feel bad for her; she didn't ask for this, and no woman deserves to live a love story in hiding. I told him it would be better if we stopped the frequent meetings to save her feelings. He said it wouldn't change a thing. He would never be able to introduce her to his family; they would always live in the shadows.

I also understood his side, being put on the spot where you have to choose to stay with the love of your life or cut ties with your family forever. The whole situation was heavy on both. I always thought about our fake wedding day; how would she feel that day, not being the one in white? Even if our marriage was just a theater to fool our families, it would still hurt her, and this was suffocating me somehow.

We had a giant event in our family. My cousin's wedding. It was a classic Lebanese wedding in São Paulo, with over 700 guests. Everyone in the family was invited; my uncle Othman, the snake aunt Lamia, and even Ziad and his family would be there. The wedding was spectacular, like something out of a fairytale. The bride wore a sparkling white dress with a crown and a giant bouquet of Colombian red roses. The hall was decorated with white and blue flowers everywhere, and the food was a massive buffet of Arab dishes. Of course, there was no alcohol because it was a Muslim wedding. The highlight was the Dabke dancing; family and friends joined a circle around the bride. All the women in the family wore long, sparkling dresses from head to toe as if it were an Oscar party. I was wearing a dark blue lace dress, and the laces were shaped like a flower. I had red lipstick on, and my hair was tight to the back. Ziad leaned over in the middle of the party and whispered, "You look stunning." I smiled, and then he continued, "You know there's another wedding happening in the ballroom next door, right? Let's check it out."

I laughed at his madness and yet agreed to the madness. We snuck out and slipped into the next ballroom. It was a Brazilian wedding that couldn't have been more different. There were only about 40 people; everyone was drinking, and the music was loud. Brazilian country songs were the ones I hated. The first thing I did was head straight to the buffet. I grabbed a pastry and took a bite, only for Ziad to yell, "That's pork!" I spit it out on the floor, horrified, and we laughed. Then he grabbed my hand and said, "Let's dance." Pushing my arm and my body to the middle of the dance floor, and I was fighting him. "No way. I don't know how to dance to Brazilian music!" pulling my arm and body backward. He kept insisting and pulling me and said he would teach me the moves. We stepped onto the dance floor, and he showed me the moves. I kept stepping on his feet and missing the rhythm, but we couldn't stop laughing; my laugh was louder than the music. His poor feet must have been sore by the end, but he didn't care; he seemed so happy, and his smile took over his whole face. Then, someone, maybe the bride's mother, walked up to us and asked suspiciously, "Do you know the bride and groom?"

Thinking fast, I answered with a pretty lie: "Yes, I used to work with the bride."

She crossed her arms and said, in a furious voice, "My daughter has never worked. Get out, or I'll call security."

We ran out of there as fast as we could, laughing like kids. On returning to my cousin's wedding, Ziad tripped and fell. He wasn't even drunk! I helped him up, and we ran back, still laughing uncontrollably. That night was one of the best of my life. It was pure fun, the memory that makes you smile whenever you think about it. At the end of my cousin's wedding, it was time for the bride to throw the bouquet. I had no interest in it, but my mom pushed me into the crowd of single women. "Go! You must catch it!" she said. I stood there awkwardly, not even trying to catch it. But somehow, the bouquet landed right in my hands. Everyone cheered, clapping and shouting and saying, "You're next! Romeo and Juliet, it's destiny!"

They were referring to Ziad and me. I looked at him, and he was laughing hysterically. He knew, just like I did, that this was all fake. I looked down at the bouquet in my hands and thought, this is not what I have been asking for. But I smiled for the crowd because I was the next bride-to-be. That same week, it was my Aunt Fatima's birthday, and my dad wouldn't let it pass quietly. He decided to take us all out to a pizza place. Not just our family; he invited Ziad's parents, too. Ziad called me later that night, saying he couldn't join us at dinner. He said loudly through the phone, "I'm meeting my girlfriend tonight. We've been fighting a lot, and it's getting worse. I'm trying to save what's left of the relationship, but it's hard. I told my parents I would work until late; say the same to yours."

I told him not to worry about anything. And do what he needs to do, and I would cover for him. At the restaurant, the vibe was wonderful. The street was alive with people, music, and laughter. The pizza place was packed, and the atmosphere was full of energy. We enjoyed laughing, sharing stories, and enjoying each other's company. As the night ended, we left the restaurant and walked down the street to find a taxi. That's when

Hamza, my younger brother, started to say while pointing ahead, "Isn't that... isn't that..."

We all turned to look at what he was pointing at, but everything seemed so normal. It was just a street full of people: some were drunk, some were cheering, and some were celebrating. There was nothing out of the ordinary.

"What are you talking about?" asked Aunt Fatima; then Walid, my older brother, said, "Oh my God, yes, it is." I followed their eyes, trying to look in the same direction as them, trying to see what they were seeing. And my heart stopped. Ziad was sitting at an outdoor bar, holding hands and leaning close to his girlfriend. Before I could react, Hamza ran towards him. "Hamza, no!" I yelled, but it was too late. Hamza reached Ziad and yanked him out of his chair, crashing to the ground. Then the punches started, along with Hamza shouting, "Are you cheating on my sister? What do you think you're doing?"

Ziad tried to explain, but Hamza wouldn't let him. Walid joined in, and the chaos began. Ziad's parents stood frozen in shock, unable to believe what they saw. I ran after them, screaming, "Stop! Let him go!" But Hamza and Walid kept shouting and hitting him with punches. "You're cheating on her! You're cheating on her!"

Finally, I screamed louder than I ever had before. "He's not cheating! We're not together! Stop it!"

The words stunned everyone. Hamza froze, his fists still clenched. Walid stopped, too. Honestly, the whole bar stopped and went silent. Everyone turned to look at me, including Ziad's parents, who seemed completely confused. I took a deep breath and said with tears in my eyes, "He's not my real boyfriend. He's not my husband-to-be. It was all pretend." The silence was unbearable. Ziad's mom looked like she was about to faint. His dad's face turned red with anger.

Then Ziad's girlfriend stood up and pointed at me, "Yes, I'm his girlfriend. She's the fake one." My dad's voice was dangerously calm. "What's going on here?" I swallowed hard and forced myself to explain, "We were pretending to be together so I could follow my dream of becoming a flight attendant. I knew you wouldn't let me, so we devised this plan. It would be a fake marriage, so you would be happy, and I could pursue my dream. I've always known about his girlfriend. He's not cheating on me because there's nothing real between us. None of this was real."

My mom's eyes filled with tears, and she said, "But you two looked so real. Like Romeo and Juliet. You looked in love!" I covered my forehead with my hands, looked down, ashamed of looking at them, and said, "No, Mama. It was all an act. Every hug and laugh was all pretend; nothing was real."

Then Ziad spoke, and with a soft voice of disappointment, he repeated my words questioningly, "Nothing was real?"

His girlfriend turned around, furious. "What do you mean, nothing? You wanted it to be real, didn't you?"

Her words sparked more shouting. Ziad's parents were horrified, his mom visibly shaking as she held onto her husband's arm. Ziad turned to my dad and said, "Please, let me come to your house. We need to talk and clear this up in private."

My dad's face was stone-cold, and he said in his selfish voice, "You're not stepping foot in my house." He grabbed my arm, pulled me towards a taxi, and pushed me inside. My family followed, leaving Ziad and his parents in the chaos. As the cab pulled away, I glanced back. Ziad was still there, his nose bleeding from Hamza's punch. He looked broken, physically and emotionally, and it tore me apart. His parents stood frozen, their faces filled with shock and humiliation. It was my fault. I had dragged him into this mess. I thought I could keep everything under control, but now everything had exploded, leaving only pain behind. When we got home, my dad's anger filled the entire house. He slammed every door he passed, kicked the furniture, and threw his keys across the living room. The tension was suffocating, and I followed behind him, my heart racing.

"Dad, please, "just let me explain. Please, Dad."

He turned around, his face red with fury, and shouted, "Explain what? Do you want to explain the humiliation you've put me through or the shame you've brought to this family? Or would you like to explain? How do you play the whole family like puppets? Making us look stupid and small in public? Why would you do this? Why would you put me in this position? Where did I go wrong with you?"

I felt tears streaming down my face as I tried to find the words; I said with trembling and fear, "You didn't do anything wrong; it's just that... I wanted to make you happy. I wanted you to be proud of me. But I also wanted to be happy too. I thought if I went through with this plan, this fake marriage, you'd be happy, and I could pursue my dream at the same time. It was going to be a win-win for everybody. I didn't think about the consequences. I know I was wrong and shouldn't have done this. But it's too late now. I can't fix it. All I can do is tell the truth. Ziad has nothing to do with this; it was all my idea. I dragged him into this mess."

Before my dad could respond, my mom stood up, her voice sharp and loud and her eyes full of hate and disgrace. "How did you have the nerve to do this with your family? Where did I go wrong while raising you? Why are you hurting us like this?"

"You didn't, Mom. You have always been by my side through thick and thin, but you should be the one who would understand me the most at this time." I continued saying with a river falling down my eyes and a heavy breath. "You had the same dream and wanted to be a flight attendant. They didn't let you. Why are you trying to force me into the same life? I don't want to end up a miserable housewife like all the women in this family."

The words were out before I could stop them, and they landed like a blow. My mom's face turned pale, and then, without warning, she raised her hand and slapped me. That slap was so strong that I could feel my cheek burning. I could feel the marks of her fingers like a tattoo on my cheek, and she continued yelling after the slap, "I didn't hurt people to make my dream come true. I put my head down when I realized I didn't have the support and saw that it wasn't possible. I obeyed my father. I didn't bring shame to my family. I didn't hurt the people I loved. You, on the other hand, have been hurting everyone around you. Look at what you've done, and for what? A dream that hasn't even come true. And I'm scared because I don't know how far you'll go for this. What else are you capable of doing to get what you want? You need to stop. Let it go. You've already tried, and it didn't work. Just stop. Stop bringing us shame. Stop hurting your family. You're tired, and you're making us tired too."

She paused, her voice softening, but the pain in her eyes was unmistakable. "We're not against you. We're not trying to hurt you or take away your happiness. We want to see you safe, loved, and cared for. We want to see you build a family, be happy, and be loved. Why would you keep jumping from one rejection to another, humiliating yourself for a job thousands of people dream of but only a small percentage ever get? What makes you think you'll be one of them? What if you spend forever trying to make it true until it's too late to find love? Find security? Find stability? What guarantee do you have that it will ever become true?"

Her words filled the room like a sandstorm. Leaving everything messy and out of place. My legs were so shaky that I couldn't stand up anymore. I fell on my knees, with my face washed with my tears. I didn't know what to say. Part of me wanted to scream back, to fight for my dream, but another part felt crushed under their disappointment and fear. I was so ashamed of what I had done that I couldn't even lift my head after the slap to look at my parents or my brothers. And there I stayed, on the floor, smashed, paying for my sins.

CHAPTER 14

The Peacock

الطاووس

Everything was still so difficult for me. After all the drama I had caused, the shame I brought to my parents, and the fights, the atmosphere at home was heavy. My dad barely spoke to me, and my mom wasn't any better. My brothers were distant, too, their sadness hanging in the air. The house felt suffocating, filled with negative energy. I couldn't escape the weight of my guilt. No matter how often I apologized, I couldn't fix what I had done. I had hurt them deeply, and I hated myself for it. All I ever wanted was to make them happy, to see them proud of me. Instead, I had failed them over and over again, chasing a dream that wasn't even coming true.

My mom echoed, "You've hurt everyone around you, and for what?"

She was right. I had destroyed relationships and caused pain, all for a dream that seemed so hard to achieve. I started showing symptoms of anxiety. At work, I'd sit at the reception desk, feeling a heavy weight on my chest. Sometimes, I'd look down at my hands and see them shaking uncontrollably. I wasn't myself anymore; I wasn't the smiling, radiant person I used to be. Something inside me had broken, and I didn't know how to fix it. Even physically, the stress was showing. Red dots would suddenly appear on my chest, coming and going without warning. My breathing felt heavy, and the nauseous feeling, as if I was a pregnant woman, was always there. At work, everyone noticed that I wasn't the same.

The energy I once had was gone, replaced by a heaviness that I couldn't bear to carry. One day, I was working on a new project on the same floor as Nanda. We were building some files, printing, and cutting a lot of papers to prepare the documents; as I cut the papers, my hands started shaking. I tried to steady them, but it wasn't working. Nanda noticed and asked me if I was okay; I said, "I'm not sure," with my eyes looking down, and she said, "I've been noticing for a while that you're not okay. And I want to tell you that it's okay not to feel okay and to ask for help."

She put the scissors down and pulled her chair closer to mine. "I've been seeing a psychologist for a while now. She's amazing. She's helped me so much in all aspects of my life, and I think she could help you, too. " She saw in my face that I wasn't really excited about her suggestion, and she continued to convince me with her huge smile and holding my hands tight.

"You don't need to be depressed or have anxiety to see someone. Sometimes, you need a person to talk to. Someone who doesn't know you, someone you can be completely honest with. It's not about weakness but about taking care of yourself." She pulled a small card out of her bag and handed it to me.

"This is her card. She's not just a psychologist but also a career coach. If you're feeling like things are heavier than they should be, go to her. She'll help you carry it or at least help you figure out how to manage it." I stared at the card, the name and number printed neatly. I put it in my purse and told her I would consider it. Later that day at work, I was in the dressing room when Thalia walked in, her face glowing with excitement. She raised her hand for a high-five and said, "I made it! I passed! I got the call. Dubai Airways has hired me!"

I stared at her in shock; then I screamed, "What?!" She still had her hand up, waiting for the high five. Our palms touched, and we both started screaming and laughing. I hugged her tightly, laughing and crying at the same time, like always, happy for her success and sad for my failure. Hugging her with that mixed feeling and with the anxiety kicking me. Then she said, "I wish you were coming with me; I'm so sorry you didn't make it. But you can still do it. You can apply as many times as you want until you get it, and you know that more than I do."

I took a deep breath and looked at her, shaking my head left and right. "Forget about it. It's not meant to be mine. You know what? Maybe my purpose in this whole thing was to meet you. Maybe I was put here to help you, not to become a flight attendant myself. That's probably why destiny brought me to this job and put you in my path. You were always the chosen one, not me."

She looked at me, her eyes full of empathy, and told me not to lose hope. Then her tone changed, and she asked me not to tell Tamara about her being hired; I didn't understand why she didn't want to share her happiness with her the same way she shared with me, and she said, "She gave me bad vibes. Every time she's around, I feel... off. I don't trust her. I know she's your friend, and I know you care about her, but please, just don't tell her."

"But she's already asking. She knows you made it to the final interview and keeps asking if you got the job." If she keeps asking, I'll tell her myself that

I didn't make it. I just don't trust her. I don't want any negativity or evil eye messing this up. I still have some medical exams to submit and some paperwork to fill; I don't want her evil eye messing up everything."

I promised Thalia that day that I wasn't going to say anything. It wasn't my place anyways. It was her happiness, her news, and it was up to her who she would like to share it with. I always felt a lot, and I never felt anything towards Tamara the way Thalia did, but this time, I decided to keep my eyes open for any red flags. Tamara worked with me on the same floor the next morning. She walked in, looking cheerful and playing with her long blonde hair; she smiled at me and said, "Did Thalia tell you she didn't get hired by Dubai Airways?"

"Oh yeah, I felt so bad for her," I said, and Tamara laughed. "I knew it! They would never hire her. She doesn't have what it takes to be a flight attendant. I don't even know what she was doing in that interview. I wanted to tell her to go home and stop wasting her time, but it wasn't my place. So, I let her embarrass herself."

She laughed again, shaking her head and clapping both hands. She continued, "Thalia's like a pigeon thrown into a cage full of peacocks. She doesn't belong in the skies. She doesn't have the glamour, the sparkle, or the personality. She barely talks; she's weird; she's not approachable. She doesn't belong in the flight attendant life. But hey, she learned her lesson. I hope she doesn't show up there again."

I felt disgusted. Tamara's words revealed a side of her I had never seen before, a side that made me understand why Thalia didn't trust her. Her negativity, arrogance, and inability to be happy for someone else's success shocked me. For the first time, I realized that Tamara wasn't the friend I thought she was. She wasn't someone who celebrated others' victories. She needed to be the best, the most perfect, and she couldn't stand the idea of someone else achieving something she hadn't. For a moment, I kept thinking about what kind of things she wished on me. Does she wish me ill? Does she make fun of me when I'm not around in front of the other girls? Does she go home and laugh about my pain with her boyfriend?

The person in front of me was mean, completely different. I didn't recognize her, or maybe she was always like this, and I was too blind or innocent to notice. Then I started to have a lot of flashbacks; it was like I had been in a coma, and I had just woken up. I started to remember her looks towards me, how she stares at me upside down, how sometimes she hugs me, but it never feels real, how she gives me life advice, but with a cold heart and sometimes always with a sarcastic comment. All the girls weren't that close to her, and she was always going to have lunch alone. Everything started to make sense. I was slowly waking up, but I still wanted to keep observing her behavior even more.

She asked me if I would like to apply again in a couple of months when Dubai Airways comes back to São Paulo, and for the first time, I decided to act like Thalia, and I only said, "I'm not sure."

Then she opened her big fat mouth, "I think it's better if you don't! Think with me... If they keep coming to São Paulo, it is because they are looking for native Portuguese speakers, and you are not a native. Maybe that's why you haven't been accepted."

First, she shames Thalia in front of me, then me, trying to put me down or convince me to give up completely on my dreams because she fears me getting there before her. I smiled gently, and I played by her rules and said, "You are right. Maybe I'm also just a pigeon among a bunch of peacocks."

CHAPTER 15

Stockholm Syndrome

متلازمة ستوكهولم

I was on my way to work, sitting quietly on the metro, when I began to notice something strange. The train was full when I boarded, but as it moved through the tunnels, it began to empty. Station after station passed, but the train didn't stop. It sped up, moving so fast it felt like a bullet train. I hold on to the pole near my seat, feeling a rising panic. Why wasn't it stopping? I asked myself. Looking around, I realized something strange: no passengers were left. The once-crowded metro was now completely empty, and I was alone. Suddenly, the train applied its brakes. The doors opened, and I hesitated for a moment before stepping out.

When I looked around, I almost had a heart attack. I was no longer in São Paulo. In front of me stood the Oriental Pearl Tower, the iconic skyscraper of Shanghai. I could feel the warm, humid air of the city, hear the cars beeping in their busy streets, and smell the aroma of street food. The details were vivid, too vivid. I wasn't just dreaming; I was there. But then I woke up. I was in my bed, drenched in sweat, my heart pounding. The dream was so real that it took me a few moments to realize it wasn't. I sat on the edge of my bed, holding my head in my hands. This wasn't normal. My desperation to become a flight attendant consumed me, haunting my every thought, even my dreams.

I couldn't go on like this. Nanda's words came back to me: "It's okay to ask for help." That day, I called the psychologist she recommended. Her name was Carol, and she sounded kind over the phone. She told me she had an opening that morning, so I booked it. It was going to be my first time talking to a psychologist. I never thought that one day I would need one. I was a very judgmental person. I thought that psychologists were only for people with suicidal thoughts or the ones who had given up completely on themselves and on life.

I didn't know what to expect when I arrived at her office. The room was cozy, with soft lighting and a warm, welcoming feel. A fluffy carpet covered the floor, and the walls were lined with bookshelves filled with thick volumes. A few potted plants added a touch of life to the space, and there was a faint scent of lavender in the air. Carol greeted me with a smile. She was a woman in her late 40s with red hair, glasses, and light skin. She started by offering me a cup of herbal tea, and I immediately accepted.

Sitting down, I noticed a box of tissues nearby, as if she expected tears. I scanned the room again, noticing the framed certificates of her professional achievements on the wall and the little touches that made the space feel safe and comfortable. After a moment, she sat across from me and said, "So, what brings you here today? I will be glad to listen and assist in every way possible."

Her voice was so smooth, and I felt an unexpected urge to open up. I told her everything: the anxiety, the shakiness, the red dots on my chest that appeared out of nowhere. I told her about my dream of becoming a flight attendant, the three failed attempts, and the mess I had made with my family and Ziad. Carol listened without interrupting, her expression never changing. When I was done, she leaned forward slightly and uttered, "It sounds like you're carrying a lot right now. Would you like to start from the beginning? Tell me about your life."

I told her I was born in Brazil, and we moved to Colombia as children and then to Lebanon to learn Arabic. I told her about growing up during the 2006 war between Lebanon and Israel, about the fear and the trauma that stayed with me long after the bombs stopped falling. About the trauma I endured at school in Lebanon for simply climbing a mountain and petting some dogs, the rumors, losing my friends, having to change schools, and the pressure of having to act like a perfect lady at my young age when I wanted to be running free, riding bikes, watching sunsets, and wearing what I wanted to wear without any restriction. My responsibility as a child was to maintain appearances and act like a lady waiting for a husband to come. We have been through financial difficulties, not having money to buy food and having to live on donations from our family members. My mom left the house to sell her gold so she didn't have to humiliate herself to her parents and ask for money. My dad had been vanishing for years without asking about us. The loss of my great grandma.

The humiliation Amer put me through by being ashamed of dating me. It was a lot to talk about, and I told her everything. Vented everything out, cried, and ran out of breath talking about my past. I told her about moving back to Brazil three years ago, my struggles to adapt, and the pressure to meet my family's expectations. I shared how I lied to my parents, my failed attempts to become a flight attendant, and how everything spiraled out of control with Ziad. Carol listened to everything, looking straight into my eyes, and then she finally said, "You've been through so much. It's no wonder you're feeling the way you are. I understand the culture you come from, the pressure to make your family happy, to follow the rules, to sacrifice your own desires for their approval. But I want you to remember something: your happiness matters too. You can't live your life for others and forget yourself."

Her words hit me deeply. I had never thought about it that way before. She gave me so much advice that day and treated me well, making me see things differently. I did feel comfortable with her, and we agreed to meet twice a week for therapy, every Monday and Thursday at the same time. Every session, we would talk about how my days were going about work, my personal life, Ziad, and things at home.

She had this safe space where I could be myself. I could talk about absolutely everything, even my darkest thoughts, without being judged. She would always recommend books to read, and they were about women's rights or self-help. Books that would lift my spirits and dive me into a new world of hope and dreams. I developed a love for reading because of her, so I started to read two books per month. It was helping me escape depression. After reading the books, I share my point of view with her and what I have learned from every story. She was the kind of therapist who didn't want me to lose myself or stop dreaming. She told me to keep trying to become a flight attendant, even if the world was against it. She would say, "If something keeps you awake at night, then it's worth chasing." Everything that I would point out as a negative thing about me would make me see it as a positive thing.

I started to love myself more. Of course, I was still scared of my parents and about making some decisions alone, but she would make everything feel lighter. She often told me, "Don't wait for people's support, motivation, or recognition to get what you want; that motivation should also come from inside you." Slowly, I was being taught how to be independent and have self-love. Weeks have passed. Therapy was helping, little by little. My anxiety wasn't gone, but it felt more manageable; it felt lighter. Having someone to share my frustration never felt so good.

One day at work, it was Tamara, Hanna, and me in the reception, each girl in front of her computer busy working, organizing meetings, and solving problems that weren't even ours; then, an email from Thalia arrived in our shared inbox. The subject line was "Farewell." In the email, Thalia announced that Dubai Airways had hired her, and she was leaving Brazil to move to Dubai and start a new career as a flight attendant. She thanked us for all the years of working together, for everything she had learned in that job, and was excited for the new chapter in her life. I looked at Tamara, who was seated just next to me, and I saw her face twisting with disbelief; then she started to shout, "This bitch told me she didn't make it!"

She repeated the phrase three times, shouting and punching the keyboard in front of her. For a second, I was terrified, and Hanna had her eyes wide open, just as shocked as I was by her reaction. Her voice rose, filled with anger and jealousy.

"That's not fair! It was supposed to be me! She doesn't have what it takes to be a flight attendant; that wasn't even her dream; it had never been her dream."

Her anger turned into an uncontrollable rage. She pulled her hair in front of us, screaming, and tears fell out of her face like a waterfall, and she continued saying while shouting, "Why? Why her and not me? This was supposed to be mine; I was supposed to be moving to Dubai, not this skinny weird bitch."

I didn't know how to calm her, nor did Hanna. Her voice was so loud, and we had meeting rooms full of international clients. Everyone was getting out of the rooms to see what was happening, but she didn't seem to care; she was extremely out of control and forgot that she was at her workplace. Then, suddenly, she stops shouting for a second and keeps staring at me. After a few seconds, she says, "You! This was all you! You took her to that interview to steal my place, and if you had kept your big mouth shut, she wouldn't have stolen my future."

She said it, pointing her finger at me and getting closer and closer. I stood up, looked her in the eyes, and said, "She didn't steal anything from you. Maybe they had too many peacocks and needed a pigeon, so it was meant to be hers."

I have never stood up for myself that way at work, and I guess therapy was really helping. And I always felt intimidated in front of Tamara. She had this air of confidence that would make anyone doubt themselves. Whenever I was around her, I agreed with everything she said, and I was always scared of speaking up or sharing a different point of view from hers. I would often feel small and vulnerable next to her. It was as if I was a candle, and she would blow off my light whenever she was around me.

She stared at me with a face of disbelief. She suddenly became pale; her eyes were wide open. I could feel she was out of control, and soon, she was going to jump on me and beat me up, but she didn't. She fainted in the reception. Hanna was just behind her and grabbed her before she hit her head on the floor. We rushed, laying her on the floor, and elevated her legs. Our manager came immediately because someone had called saying there was a scandal in the reception. She saw Tamara faint on the floor and called a medical team. She was taken straight to a hospital, leaving everyone in that law firm shocked with her reaction. It was like she showed her true colors, who she really was, a personality full of hate and jealousy hidden under the carpet for years.

After the tumultuous events with Tamara at the reception, I eagerly anticipated my therapy session with Carol. She had become my confidante, always ready to listen to the dramas and adventures of the law firm and my life.

She was there for my moments of depression, happiness, complaints, and blessings. The day of our session arrived, and I went to her office. I began recounting the incident with Tamara and how she reacted to Thalia's success, revealing a side of her that I had never seen before. I expressed my shock and disappointment, realizing that Tamara wasn't the genuine friend I had believed her to be. I couldn't keep someone with such negativity in my life; she drained my energy and dimmed my light.

During our conversation, Carol received an unexpected call and had to step out to get it. I was left alone, so I wandered around the room, examining the books on her shelves, which were beautifully organized, smelling the flowers and the plants she had on the table, and having a brief look at the certificates of her achievements as a psychologist and career coach adorning the walls. By her desk, I noticed a book that caught my attention. It was a Torah, the Jewish holy book, translated into Portuguese. Confused, I wondered why she had it. When Carol returned, I asked if she was studying religion. She replied, "No." I then asked her about the Torah on her desk, asking if it was a gift. She looked at me calmly and said, "I'm Jewish."

Her words hit me like a bullet. I felt a surge of emotions: betrayal, confusion, and anger. I had been pouring my heart out to her, sharing my deepest traumas, including those from the war involving Israel, and she was Jewish. I couldn't comprehend it. I confronted her, accusing her of betrayal. I stood up, brutally distancing myself from her. "You should have told me; I've been pouring my heart out about the war, about my nightmares, and all this time, you were one of them," I said to her with a disappointed voice.

Carol remained calm, her voice steady as she responded, "I am not one of them. I haven't harmed you or anyone else. My religion is a part of who I am, just as yours is a part of you. I didn't disclose it because this space is about you, not me. And you never asked."

Her words made sense, yet the volcano inside of me was erupting. I mumbled an excuse and hurried out of the office, anger blurring my vision. The revelation had reopened old wounds, and I felt lost, unsure how to process this new information. The next day at work, I confronted Nanda, accusing her of withholding information. She stood up, ready to fight and defend herself, insisting she had no idea about Carol's faith. She reminded me that such personal details aren't typically discussed in professional appointments. She said she would never send a Muslim with a bunch of traumas like mine to shake hands with a Jew. She promised that she never knew, asked, or cared about our psychologist's fate. She stated that she doesn't go around asking people what they believe in because this kind of subject never mattered to her, and then she said, "Listen, Arabic, you must let go of these prejudices, and Carol has been helping you. Her religion doesn't define her character or her ability to support you."

Nanda's words were like a shock of reality in my mind, and I began to reflect on my reaction. Carol had been supportive, guiding me through some of the darkest periods of my life. Her faith had never influenced the compassion and professionalism she extended toward me, yet I was simultaneously so angry and confused. The amount of trauma I have had because of the war. I grew up listening to that Jewish people are bad people, that they always wanted to steal our land, blow up our houses, and kill our people, and then suddenly there I was, opening up to one. I felt like I was raising a snake, letting her starve so she could eat me alive.

Days passed, and I was distracted by my thoughts. Carol had been instrumental in my progress. She had shown me kindness, understanding, and guidance. Could I let her faith overshadow the help she provided? On Thursday, I decided to return to her, but I found myself standing outside her office, my heart pounding. She welcomed me warmly, expressing her gladness at my return.

I sat, took a deep breath, and then told her about something I learned in my flight attendant course: the word "Stockholm Syndrome." It is when the hijacker puts the victim's life in danger and then removes the threat that the victim starts to develop a feeling of empathy towards the hijacker for removing the threat, and this turns into a syndrome called Stockholm. And that is how I felt towards her. I felt like I was experiencing Stockholm Syndrome, developing an attachment to someone I perceived as a threat.

She gently corrected me, stating she was neither a hijacker nor a threat. She acknowledged the historical conflicts between our peoples but emphasized that she wasn't responsible for the actions of others. Just as I wasn't accountable for the actions of all Muslims, and she wasn't for all Jews. She asked me to see beyond religion, to see the person as a human being with a soul and feelings, and not to see only religion. I realized that judging someone's principles and personality based on religion was an injustice. Carol had been nothing but supportive.

We hugged, and I apologized for my reaction. She reassured me of her unconditional support, regardless of my choices or beliefs. This experience taught me the importance of looking beyond labels and prejudices. It reminded me that humanity transcends religious and cultural boundaries, and genuine connections can be found in the most unexpected places. Just like that, she taught me how to see things differently and learn to like and love people despite their religion or gender. She proved to me that Muslims and Jews can be together in the same room, have a conversation, and help each other. She and I were proof of that because we made it happen. We were not responsible for the killings, for the traumas, or for decisions taken by governments that make civilians pay the price for the rest of their lives. She never killed anyone, and neither did I. We were just two humans with hearts and feelings, with different religions, full of life, dreams, and love to share.

CHAPTER 16

Inshallah

إن شاء الله

The day had finally come. Thalia was leaving São Paulo to start her new life in Dubai, and Paulina and I were at the airport to say goodbye. We stood together in front of the check-in area, surrounded by the noise of people coming and going, people hugging each other, some with happy faces and others with tears in their eyes, lovers kissing goodbye. Some had backpacks ready for their new solo adventure, but everything happening around us didn't matter at that moment. It was just the three of us saying our last words before she left and praying for the clock to slow down so we could stay with her as much as we could. It was emotional for all of us.

For me, because I was at the airport, a place I had always dreamed of being, a place I wanted to pass through as part of something bigger. For Paulina, it was special because she used to work for Dubai Airways, and being here brought back so many memories for her. And for Thalia, it was the start of something new.

A life she would have never imagined she would have; she was going to live in a place where thousands of people wished to be living: Dubai, the city of dreams. While we stood there, something caught our attention. A group of flight attendants working for Dubai Airways entered the terminal, walking together like they owned the place. Their high heels clicked loudly on the floor, all in perfect rhythm. They looked so professional in their brown uniforms, their scarves tied perfectly around their necks, and their red lipstick made them stand out even more. They were wonderful. Every detail about them was perfect: how they walked, the way they carried themselves, even the way they dropped their bags at the counter, ready to check in for their flight.

I couldn't stop looking at them. They were everything I wanted to be. I wished I was one of them, walking confidently through the airport, ready to fly back to Dubai. But it wasn't me. It was Thalia. She was going to join them, not me. Thalia turned to me and smiled with tears in her eyes at the same time. She must have seen how I looked at them because she said, "Arabic, your time is going to come. One day, you'll be here, walking like them, dragging your suitcase, wearing the scarf and the red lipstick. You'll hear your heels clicking on this floor, just like theirs. And I know you'll fly passengers back to Dubai and worldwide. Your time will come."

I looked at her, tears in my eyes, and said, "Inshallah." That was all I could say because I was so overwhelmed by emotion. We hugged each other tightly. I couldn't stop crying. She held my hands and started her regret speech: "I wish I had been closer to you. I'm sorry I was so focused on my world and did not have an opportunity to get to know you. I wish we had more time to enjoy our friendship. But I know we'll meet again in Dubai. It's going to be home for both of us."

"Inshallah," I whispered again, my voice breaking. Paulina hugged her, too, and we all cried. Then the time came for Thalia to go. We waved at her as she walked toward the gate. She turned back one last time to look at us and then disappeared into the restricted area. She was gone. I stood there, still crying. Paulina put her arms around me to comfort me. She said softly, "Don't worry, your time will come. One day, we will be back here, and I will be saying goodbye to you; it will be your time to shine in Dubai; I know it, I feel it."

"I don't think so, Paulina," I said. I'm just meant to help others achieve their dreams. Maybe I wasn't meant to be a flight attendant. Maybe that's why God put me in her life, to guide her, not to live the dream myself; it was always meant to be hers, never mine."

Paulina hugged me tightly while my tears fell and said, "Just say it, habibty (my love), say Inshallah. You know how powerful that word is."

I took a deep breath, closed my eyes, and said it again. "Inshallah."

It was a new day, and I went to work as usual. When I got to the reception, the girls were there. Tamara was back, too. She had been out of work for a while after her hysterical breakdown when she found out that Thalia got into Dubai Airways, and she didn't. Looking at her, I could feel the anger radiating from her. Her expression was sharp, full of negativity. It was as if poison was dripping from her face. For the first time, I understood what Thalia had always warned me about when she said, "Don't trust her." Then Sara shared the big news she heard in the hallways with the team, breaking the silence.

"They're hiring a new receptionist to replace Thalia. We'll need to train her and teach her everything."

Then Tamara adds her comment with a sarcastic smile and poison in her heart: "Well, I don't think she'll give us too much trouble. I'm sure she speaks Portuguese perfectly. And she's not coming from planet Mars and attached to alien traditions, right?"

I knew she was talking about me, mocking me. She was still bitter because I was the one who introduced Thalia to the world of flight attendants and convinced her to try the interview. But I didn't respond. I just looked at her and stayed quiet. She didn't stop there. She turned to me again. "Did you hear? A new girl is coming. Are you planning to take her to the next Dubai Airways interview? Going to make her the next flight attendant, too?"

Her tone was filled with anger and poison, yet I refrained from reacting to her. I ignored her again. Eventually, she left for her break. Sara went with her, and it was just me, Hanna, and Mariana left at reception. That's when the girls said they needed to talk to me. They looked serious, as if they had been holding this revelation in for a long time; they said it was a subject they had been having trouble letting go of for months. I was confused but asked them to continue; then Mariana said, "When you had that interview at the aviation school, did you leave your bag in the reception while you went to the toilet? And Tamara was on the same floor?"

I nodded. "Yes, that's what happened. Why?" Hanna continued, "And you're sure you put your ID in your bag before you went to the bathroom, right?" Yes," I said. "I was positive it was there. But it was gone when I got to the interview; my irresponsibility that day still bothers me." The two of them exchanged a look before they spoke again. Then Mariana strikes, "Have you ever thought about the possibility that Tamara was the one who took your ID out of your bag?"

The question shocked me. "No, I've never thought of that. Do you think she would really do something like that?" Hanna stood up, her voice rising with frustration, and she had her diva attitude as usual. "For God's sake! Nesrin, did you see how she acted when Thalia entered Dubai Airways? She screamed, hit things, and pulled her hair. That was not normal! What leads you to believe she didn't have similar negative thoughts about you? What makes you think she wouldn't try to destroy your dream, too?"

Mariana joined in, her voice full of conviction. "Do you remember when we suggested checking the security footage? Do you remember how defensive she got? She told us it was a waste of time and tried to make us feel like we were crazy. Looking back, it's so obvious. She didn't want us to see the cameras because they would have shown her taking your ID out of your bag, ruining your chance to become a flight attendant."

At that moment, I was already convinced that it was Tamara. After everything I had seen and witnessed, there was no doubt that she had hijacked my future. I didn't need any proof; her actions would speak for themselves.

"Maybe you're right, and it's not impossible. But I can't prove it, and I'm not going to confront her. I would rather not accuse her without evidence. If she did it, karma would take care of her."

Hanna and Mariana nodded, but I could see the anger lingering on their faces. As for me, I decided to let it go. Their theory was right, and I was convinced Tamara had done it. But there was no point in holding onto it now. What was meant for me would come in its time. And I told them that the only thing left was to let karma do her job because if I have learned something in life, we collect what we plant. If she planted poisoned fruits, sooner or later, she would starve and end up eating her own fruits. Later that day, one of the meeting rooms was full of international lawyers. They had just finished a big meeting. After every meeting, it was our job to quickly clean the room and prepare it for the next one. Hanna said, "I'll go clean that meeting room because I know they had a lot of food. They had a big catering setup with sandwiches. I will grab some sandwiches for us to eat at reception."

She returned to the room holding a bunch of sandwiches hidden inside an envelope; that was how we usually took food from the meetings. She brought them over, and it was me, her, and Tamara at the reception desk later that day. I grabbed one of the sandwiches and started eating it. It was so good, one of the best sandwiches I'd ever had. "Oh my God, this is delicious!" I said. Hanna laughed. "Of course! It's ham." As soon as she said that, I spit out the sandwich immediately, realizing I had already eaten half of it.

"Oh my God! Why is this meeting always full of haram sandwiches?" I said in a frustrated voice. "Sorry, I can't keep up with this; I always forget you can't eat pork." Said Hanna, her voice filled with guilt and apology. Then Tamara turned to me and said with her mean girl face, staring at me up and down, and with poison coming out of the side of her mouth:

"Why can't you eat pork? Is it because your Allah used to raise pigs as one of his kids?" I stared at her in shock. Her comment was so racist, so hurtful, so Islamophobic. She was making fun of my religion. She could have joked about anything: my hair, my attitude, my family, but not my faith. That was crossing a line. Hanna immediately spoke up. "What you said is Islamophobic, Tamara. That's not right, and you shouldn't joke like that."

I looked at Tamara and said firmly, "I've had enough And this time, I have witnesses. I can't prove that you were the one who stole my ID from my bag, but this is vivid proof of your racism.

Without wasting any time, I went straight to the manager's office. I opened the door and explained everything that had just happened. I told her about the Islamophobic joke Tamara had made and how it wasn't the first time I had faced something like this. I made it clear this was a serious issue and shouldn't be ignored, especially in a law firm as respected as ours. There were witnesses; Hanna was there to back me up, and I knew she would have my back. Security cameras in the reception area would have caught everything Tamara said. The manager promised to take it seriously, and they immediately started an investigation. The next thing I knew, Tamara was suspended from work. They reviewed the camera footage and questioned Hanna, who confirmed everything. Tamara, on the other hand, kept denying it. She insisted she never said anything like that, but the evidence was against her. In the end, she was fired.

I never saw her again after that. When she was fired, security escorted her out of the building. She wasn't allowed to leave on her own. She had to go through HR and sign all her termination papers, and then security walked her to the exit. From that moment on, she was banned from returning to the office. As she left, Hanna looked at me and said

"I guess she ate the poisoned fruits she planted." This was the last time any of us saw her. That day was her last day at work. Her last mean joke, her last way of putting people down. I felt bad and never wanted to make anyone lose their job. But I couldn't live a life being stepped on all the time. She never wished me well or any of the girls. She had a dark soul that would feed on people's hopes and dreams; it was draining. Everything we lived together was all a lie. She was never a friend. She was a snake pretending to be a butterfly, ready to eat you when she starved. I believed in karma, and it did finally catch her.

CHAPTER 17

Mabrouk

مبروك

I received a message from my cousin Rayan in Lebanon. She told me her wedding was coming up soon. She was marrying a man she had been introduced to by my aunt Rufaida and my uncle Mosab. They had known each other for about two weeks, decided they liked each other, got engaged, and now they were about to take the next step. It all happened quickly, but this is how most marriages happen in Lebanon, especially in villages like ours. Rayan had always been by my side while I was growing up. We shared everything: our lives, our secrets, even our social media passwords, and all our memories.

I knew how much it hurt her when I moved to Brazil and left her behind. We both missed each other every single day. So, when she told me about her wedding, I knew I had to be there for her. I applied for vacation at the law firm, and when it was approved, I felt ready to pack my bags and head back to Lebanon. At that time, my dream of becoming a flight attendant was something I had pushed far from my mind. It just wasn't working out. I was convinced that it wasn't meant to be. Dubai Airways had announced another round of interviews in São Paulo, but I didn't even bother signing up. I told myself I was done chasing something that never seemed to work out. Instead, life had started shifting in a different direction.

I was beginning to get to know someone, a guy named Malik. He was Lebanese, like me, and we were starting to connect, though it was still early. Malik was open-minded, respectful, and kind, and we got along well. He wasn't some random stranger either; our families knew each other. His father had been best friends with my dad for years, and my dad was so happy for Malik and me; he had always loved him. But even though everything seemed fine, I wasn't sure if this was what I truly wanted. It was a long-distance relationship, and my heart felt empty. I shared all of this with my therapist, Carol. She listened patiently but seemed unsure, too.

"Are you sure this is what you want?" She asked me more than once. Are you sure you want to give up on your dream and start a family? You are only 21. Can't this wait?"

I explained to her that 21 years old wasn't early in my culture. And I was getting old because my cousins and friends were already getting married before that age. In my culture, the older you get, the harder it gets to get married. I also felt pressure from all sides, including my family, aunts, and grandparents. Everybody was waiting for the day they finally got to say "Mabrouk" to me, which means congratulations in Arabic.

I also told her that I didn't know what I wanted anymore. My dream, which I built my whole life around, didn't work out. So now I'm just following my parents' advice. They keep telling me not to wait around, meet someone, or build a family. That could be what my future is meant to be. That could be what's written for me. I bid Carol farewell and told her we would continue our sessions once I returned from Lebanon. My mom and I packed our bags, and soon, we were flying to Lebanon. It felt strange to be heading back, not as the same person I was when I left, but as someone still figuring out where her life was going.

We flew to Lebanon with Dubai Airways. Boarding that plane was an experience I'll never forget. I saw the girls in the uniforms I had always dreamed of wearing everywhere I looked. Their perfect red lipstick, neatly tied scarves, and graceful smiles made them look glamorous. They walked up and down the aisle, serving drinks and food, traveling the world, and living the life I had wanted so badly. As I sat there, watching them, I felt mixed emotions. I felt like I had worn this uniform in a past life. It felt wrong to be seated as a passenger and not working. But there was also a sense of acceptance creeping in; I had to accept my reality. Sitting next to me, my mom noticed me staring at them. She gently held my hand and said, "You tried. You tried so many times, and it didn't work. Don't be so hard on yourself. Things happen when God wants them to happen. Maybe this wasn't meant for you. We never know."

Her words brought tears to my eyes, but I didn't say anything. I just nodded and looked out the window. Our flight had a stopover in Dubai before continuing to Lebanon, and once again, it was Dubai Airways. The same beautiful uniforms, the same elegant flight attendants. I couldn't stop thinking about what it would feel like to be one of them, drag my suitcase through the airport, wear red lipstick, and be part of their world. But I pushed the thought aside. I told myself it was time to move on. As we approached Beirut, I looked out the window. The view of Lebanon took my breath away.

The big Al Raouche Rocks, the sea, and the sparkling blue water—it was stunning. The landing was smooth, and its beauty overwhelmed me. I started to cry. Lebanon had always been a place I loved deeply. The country, the mountains, the fresh air, and the smell of flowers were magical. But my village? That was a different story. I never felt like I belonged there; the people often made me feel small. Still, being back in the country and seeing its beauty brought so many emotions rushing to the surface. I missed it. I missed home. I missed my cousins, my family, and the memories. It had been three and a half years since I left Lebanon. I was just a hopeless girl when I left, but now I was returning as a completely different person. Brazil had changed me in ways I couldn't explain. It changed my mindset, my attitude, and how I saw the world. I was nervous about how my family would see the new me. When we arrived at my family's house, all my worries disappeared. Everyone welcomed us with huge smiles and warm hugs. The table was covered with food and a massive buffet to celebrate our arrival.

The energy in the house was full of happiness, and I felt so loved. The news didn't take long to spread: "I was talking to Malik." My mom had made sure everyone knew, so the excitement in the room doubled. People kept saying I was the next bride-to-be. They teased me with their jokes about marriage and homemakers. I laughed with them, but I wasn't sure how I felt deep down. Was that what I wanted? To be the next bride? To settle down? I didn't know. But at that moment, I let their excitement carry me. It was a time to celebrate and enjoy the time with my family.

One morning, I woke up to the sound of birds singing outside my window. That's how peaceful and beautiful my village was. My room overlooked the lake; the sunlight streaming made everything warm and calm. When I got out of bed, I found my grandmother had already set the breakfast table. It was a proper Lebanese breakfast; everything was fresh and was homemade. There was labneh, zaatar, manakish, olives straight from the trees in our garden, and tomatoes freshly picked that morning. The Arabic tea was warm, fragrant, and perfect.

Sitting there at the table with my grandmother, surrounded by all the familiar tastes and smells, I felt like I was home in every sense. I had missed this vibe so much. As we ate, my phone buzzed. It was a message from Thalia. She told me Dubai Airways was coming to Lebanon to hire cabin crew. All their employees had been told to spread the news, especially to Arabic speakers. They were specifically looking for Lebanese candidates who were fluent in Arabic. Thalia sounded excited as she wrote, saying, "You're already in Lebanon, and they need Arabic speakers. This is a sign from the universe; you have to go. You must try! "

Her words hit me hard. For a moment, I thought about it, about going, about trying again. But then reality sank in, and I replied to her text, "It's impossible, Thalia. I'm talking to Malik now and don't want to disappoint my parents again. They're happy I'm considering settling down, and I don't want to ruin that. Plus, the interview is in Beirut, and I'm two hours away in the village. It's not that simple."

She didn't give up. She sent another message, practically begging me to go. "Please, Nesrin, this is your dream. Could you not give up on it? Remember what I told you; I'm waiting for you. Dubai is our home. I'm waiting for you to join me in our home."

Her words triggered something inside me. Deep down, I knew she was right. This was my dream, the dream I had pushed aside, the dream I had convinced myself wasn't mine anymore. But I didn't know what to do. Should I try again, or should I keep following the path I was on, the one my parents had pushed all those years to follow? I sat at the breakfast table, staring at my phone, caught between two worlds. Rayan sat with us at breakfast that morning, enjoying all the delicious food my grandmother had prepared. I grabbed her hand, pulled her into my bedroom, and locked the door behind us. She looked at me, confused.

"I need to talk to you," I said. I just got a message from my friend Thalia, who became a flight attendant. She told me that Dubai Airways is coming to Lebanon to hire flight attendants. And now, I don't know what to do." Rayan's eyes completely opened, and she whispered so no one would overhear our deadly conversation.

"Are you crazy? You're talking to a guy the whole family knows. Malik's family is close to ours, and everyone's already expecting you two to get engaged. You can't go to that interview. They'll kill you if they find out! You know how they'll react."

Her words hit me hard, and I felt the tears coming. I sat down on the bed, put my hands over my face, and started crying uncontrollably. I couldn't stop. Rayan sat beside me, trying to calm me down, but I couldn't hold back. Through my tears, I told her, "I'm so confused. I feel divided between two worlds. I thought I buried this dream, but I can't. It's stronger than me. I can't let it go, and it's like an obsession."

Rayan stayed quiet for a moment, then said, "We need to talk to Aunt Rufaida. She'll understand. She's the least strict of all of them and always listens."

We called Aunt Rufaida, who was seated with the rest of the family at the breakfast table. She interrupted her breakfast and asked her to come to the bedroom. We locked the door and explained everything to her as soon as she entered. The message from Thalia was about my dream of becoming a flight attendant and my family's expectations of me. She listened patiently, her expression calm and understanding. After I finished talking, she said, "Listen, if you want your answer, there's only one way to get it: Pray. You'll find your answer through prayer. There's a prayer called Salat al-Istikhara. It's a prayer Muslims do when they're unsure about something and need guidance. Here's what you'll do: wash yourself, do wudu, and pray. At the end of the prayer, you'll say the Istikhara phrase and ask God what you're confused about and what you need help with. After that, you'll wait. The next day, you might have a dream or feel a sense of clarity about what you should do. That's how God will send you a sign and guide you to the right path."

Her words brought a strange sense of peace. I decided to follow her advice. This could be how I would finally figure out what to do, whether to let my dream go forever or take one last chance. Later that night, after everyone had gone to bed, I decided to do exactly what my Aunt Rufaida had told me. I was going to perform the Salat al-Istikhara prayer. It was quiet in the house, and I felt a mixture of nervousness and hope. I wasn't sure how to perform it, so I Googled it. I read through step-by-step instructions, trying to make sure I understood everything. I even wrote down the exact words I was supposed to say at the end of the prayer, asking God for guidance. I prepared myself carefully, washing and doing wudu as if every step mattered more than ever. Then, in the quiet of my room, I stood to pray. My heart was racing. I didn't know what to expect, but I knew I had to fully open my heart and trust that God would hear and guide me. At the end of the prayer, I read the words I had written down, asking for clarity.

"O Allah, I seek Your counsel through Your knowledge, and I seek Your assistance through Your might, and I ask You from Your immense favor, for verily You alone decree our fate while I do not, and You know while I do not, and You alone possess all knowledge of the Unseen. O Allah, if You know this matter (me becoming a flight attendant) to be good for me about my religion, my life and livelihood, and the end of my affairs, my present and future, then decree it for me and facilitate it for me, and then place blessing for me within it, and if You know this affair to be harmful to me concerning my religion, my life and livelihood and the end of my affairs, then remove it from me and remove me from it, and decree for me what is good, wherever it may be, and make me content with it.'"

I poured out my confusion to God, explaining how torn I felt between my dream and my family's expectations, between what I thought I wanted and what I thought I should do. I asked for a sign, for something to show me if this was the right path or not. When I finished, I sat quietly on my prayer mat, my hands still on my knees, and I let the silence surround me. I didn't know what would happen next, but I felt lighter, as if the weight I'd been carrying had shifted slightly. I whispered one last Inshallah before going to bed, hoping I would have my answer by morning or sometime soon.

After performing the Salat al-Istikhara prayer that night, I had a dream. It was short, only a few seconds, but it felt so vivid that I could still feel it when I woke up. In the dream, my great-grandmother, who had passed away years ago, was with me. She grabbed my hand, and we were running together. She was pulling me behind her, leading me through an airport.

She was running ahead, holding my hand tightly, as if we were about to catch a plane. That was it. That was the entire dream. But when I woke up, I immediately knew it was a sign from God. I was meant to go. I couldn't explain it, but something inside me just knew. Without wasting time, I called my Aunt Rufaida and told her, my voice shaking with excitement.

"I had a dream. It was our grandma. She was pulling me through an airport. That must mean something, doesn't it?"

My aunt didn't hesitate and said confidently, "That's your sign. Start getting ready. Print out your CV. Make sure you have your photos ready. I'll talk to your Uncle Mosab, and he'll take you to the interview tomorrow."

I felt a rush of emotions: excitement, nervousness, and hope. I couldn't believe this was actually happening. But at the same time, I knew I had to keep this to myself. Malik couldn't know, and I wasn't ready to tell anyone. This was my moment, and I wouldn't let anyone stop me. My heart raced as I gathered my documents and prepared for the next day. This dream, this opportunity, it felt like it was finally time for me to take a chance again, no matter how scared or uncertain I felt. I just had to create a plan to escape Malik for the whole day. Going to that interview in Beirut would take the whole day, and he would wonder where I would be. I couldn't tell him the truth; he would break up our future engagement the same minute, and I would disappoint my parents and give my dad a heart attack. The next morning, Rayan burst into my room and shook me to wake up. I opened my eyes, rubbed them, and sat up. Then, Rayan said seriously but with a hint of relief, "We don't need an excuse anymore. A family member passed away, and everyone will be at the funeral today, so all you have to do is tell Malik that you'll be busy with the family the entire day. That's it. No one will notice you're gone. We'll go to Beirut and make your dream come true."

At first, I felt a pang of guilt. I wasn't very close to the relative who had passed, but using his funeral as an excuse felt wrong. Still, I realized it was my only chance to leave the village unnoticed. So, I told Malik I would be at the funeral all day and likely wouldn't have my phone on me. He didn't ask questions, and I felt relief and guilt. Soon after, I got into the car with Uncle Mosab and Rayan and headed to Beirut. The drive felt surreal. I couldn't believe I was going to try again. When we arrived, the scene was overwhelming. The auditorium was packed with at least 400 or 500 people. There were so many hopeful faces, and the room couldn't hold everyone. I realized we had arrived late, so I quickly handed over my CV to one of the interviewers. Unlike the interviews in São Paulo, there were no group dynamics or tests. It was a simple and quick exchange of words. The interviewer asked me a few questions.

"Do you live in Lebanon?" "No, I'm currently living in São Paulo," I replied. How many languages do you speak? Four. "Are you here on vacation?" "Yes," I said. She smiled and asked me, "If you're hired, can you stay here and join the company from Lebanon?"

I said yes without any hesitation. And she said they would let me know the outcome, and that was it. The entire interaction lasted no more than 10 minutes. As we left the auditorium, I felt unsure. It had been so fast, almost rushed. But I held onto hope. On the way back to the village, I kept thinking about the possibility of finally hearing good news. Days passed, and I checked my email constantly, refreshing my inbox over and over. But nothing came. No email. No call. Nothing. I started to feel the familiar weight of disappointment creeping in. I regretted going all the way to Beirut and trying one more time. Maybe I was chasing something that was never meant for me. My engagement was approaching, yet I had no answer from the Dubai Airways third party of recruiters. Then, one evening, Uncle Mosab came to me and said

"I spoke to a friend whose son just made it to the final interview for Dubai Airways. He told me something important about the open day you went to. Darling, you weren't supposed to leave the auditorium. After the first stage, they call out the names of the people who pass and move to the second stage immediately. You had to stay."

I stared at him, frozen, and said tremblingly, "What? That's not how it works in Brazil. In São Paulo, they send an email if you pass. I didn't know I had to stay and wait for my name to be called; the recruiter only said, "We will let you know. It never crossed my mind that she meant to let me know on the spot."

Mosab nodded gently. "That's how they do it here. You missed your chance if your name was called and you weren't there."

The realization hit me like a wave. What if they had called my name? What if I had passed? I would never know the outcome of it because I left when I wasn't supposed to. My chest felt heavy, and tears filled my eyes. I completely lost it. In front of Uncle Mosab and Aunt Rufaida, I started pulling my hair like Tamara did when she lost control. I couldn't stop myself. "That's it!" I screamed. "This isn't meant to be mine. Don't you see? I don't know why I had that dream with my great-grandmother. I don't know why I even tried. It's not meant for me. It's never been mine!"

Aunt Rufaida tried to calm me down, but I couldn't. The frustration, disappointment, and hopelessness all came crashing down at once. The dream I thought was a sign now felt like a cruel joke. I had tried many times, but the answer was always the same: this wasn't my destiny. After the incident in Beirut, I made a decision. I completely removed the idea of becoming a flight attendant from my mind. I couldn't keep holding onto something that wasn't meant for me. I burned everything: my CVs, the photos I'd taken for interviews, applications, and even the blogs and books I had read for inspiration were deleted from my computer. I even burned letters I had written to myself in my diary, promising that I would one day wear that uniform. I let it all go because I finally knew it wasn't for me. Instead, I turned my focus to Malik. He was a good man, respectful and caring. I could tell he was developing real feelings for me and believed I was the right person to build a family with. He wanted stability, a partner, and a future, and I promised myself to him and my parents. So, I agreed to the engagement.

On the day of the engagement, I wore a long blue dress. My parents, of course, made sure my shoulders were covered; they wanted everything to be done the proper way. The house was full of joy and celebration. My family surrounded me, throwing flowers and calling out, "Mabrouk! Mabrouk!" when the ring was finally around my finger. Everyone was smiling, laughing, and so happy for me. For a moment, I let myself enjoy it. The love and excitement in the air felt comforting. But deep down, a part of me couldn't ignore the quiet sadness. This wasn't the life I had dreamed of; it was the life that was available to me, the one I had to accept. The very next day was Rayan's wedding. The timing felt surreal; my engagement was followed immediately by her big day. I attended the wedding with my new fiancé, standing beside him as Rayan celebrated her happiness. It was a beautiful day filled with dancing, laughter, and family.

For a brief moment, I let myself believe this was the start of something good, but then my vacation ended. It was time to leave Lebanon and return to São Paulo. My return wasn't just a goodbye to my family but the beginning of a new chapter. I had to go back to resign from my job, pack my belongings, and prepare to leave the life I had built behind. I had to start packing my bag for my new life, a life that would take me from Miss to Mrs. My name, my identity, everything was about to change. It wasn't the life I had asked for. It wasn't the dream I had chased. But it was the life that was in front of me, and I told myself I had to accept it.

CHAPTER 18

Fighting For a Dream

القتال من اجل حلم

I returned to Brazil with a ring on my finger and a plan in my head. I had about three months to get everything in order: resign from my job, organize my life, and prepare to leave Brazil for good. My suitcase wasn't for the life I had once dreamed of, traveling the world as a flight attendant. No, this suitcase was for a different life as a housewife and a wife to Malik. I told myself this was the path I needed to follow, even if it wasn't the one I had wanted. Slowly, I started buying the things I would need. Each item I added to the suitcase felt like a piece of my dream slipping further away. But I told myself it was okay. This was my reality now, and my dream had to be buried just like my mom's. One day, I got a message on my phone. It was from Ziad, someone I hadn't spoken to in a while. "I saw your pictures on Facebook. I know you're engaged, but I don't believe it. This engagement won't last because this isn't what you want."

I ignored the message. But Ziad didn't stop there. A few days later, he sent another one. "Have you broken up with him yet? Because he's not the one for you." Again, I didn't reply. I thought if I ignored him, he would eventually stop. Then, one day, everything changed. I was leaving work, stepping outside as usual, and there he was, standing right in front of me, waiting for me. My heart raced. I couldn't believe he was there. I walked toward him, panicking, and said, "What are you doing here? Ziad, you need to stop sending messages and chasing me. I'm engaged now; that's the path I have chosen for myself; you need to leave now."

He didn't move. He looked at me, calm but determined, and said, "I'm not here to make trouble for you. I just want to talk. I have missed our days and our chats, and I have missed you. I broke up with my girlfriend after the bar incident. My parents were right, and she was not the one. We were from two different worlds, which wouldn't work, but I'm not here to cry to you about my problems; I'm here to understand why you are ruining your life."

I didn't know what to say, and he didn't stop. "I'm also here because I miss every second I spent with you. I know that for you, it didn't mean anything; it was all pretend, but I developed feelings after getting to know you. For a moment, I wished that everything was real. I love you, but more than that, I want to see you happy. I want to see you well. And you're not well; you're giving up on what you want, and I can't stand by and watch you do that."

I stood before him, begging him to stop the nonsense talking. And telling him that whatever he felt for me had to be buried, just like my dreams. He was in the past, just like my dream of flying around the world. I was committed to someone who truly loved me and was waiting for me on the other side of the world. I felt like he wasn't listening to anything I was saying. He wouldn't move or leave, and he kept insisting on me fighting for my dream.

"I'm giving you two choices, Nesrin. Either you break up with him and marry me instead, or you don't marry either of us and become a flight attendant like you have always dreamed about. I'm not letting you move to Lebanon to marry someone you don't love to please society."

His words hit me like a storm. I didn't know how to respond. I realized the mess I had caused by creating that marriage between us. He had developed feelings towards me, and that was never part of our deal back then. He couldn't stand the fact of me giving up on my dream and, at the same time, ending up with another man who wasn't him. I did have feelings for him, too; I missed him, his hugs, his support, and his charming way of making me forget my troubles and make things sound easier. But I couldn't tell him that, because I had a wedding band on my finger. The way he wanted me to keep fighting for my dream was enchanting. For the first time in a long time, I felt a spark of something I thought I had buried: "hope."

But I didn't want to go against my parents, not again. I told him he was crazy and that he needed to forget me. I told him I had hurt a lot of people, and one of those people was our parents, and they didn't deserve that, and I told him about me burning my diary with all my dreams and feelings written on it. How I deleted all the files I used to prepare for the interview. How I had exchanged a Dubai suitcase for a honeymoon suitcase. And my decision to bury that dream forever, just like my mom did to hers. I walked to the metro station and left him there; I didn't dare to look back because if I did, I would run to his arms, which wouldn't be fair to Malik and wouldn't be ethical. Ziad was different from all the guys I had met. He was someone who would move mountains to see me happy. But my happiness meant pain to others, and I had to let it go.

The days were passing so quickly, and with each one, I felt myself sinking deeper into unhappiness. I started to realize that I wasn't truly happy with my life because this wasn't the life I had wanted for myself. The weight of making everyone around me happy while ignoring my needs and dreams began crushing me. I wanted to escape, to run away, to disappear, and start a new life. But I couldn't. I didn't dare to bring my parents down again, to disappoint them one more time. So, I stayed. I smiled when expected to, nodded when people talked about my future as Malik's wife, and pretended I was fine. But inside, I was slowly dying. The symptoms started to creep back, the same ones I thought I'd left behind. The anxiety returned, the red dots appeared on my skin, and my appetite vanished. Whenever I tried to eat, I couldn't keep the food down. My body was rejecting everything.

My hair started to fall out in clumps, and every time I brushed it, I felt more of myself slipping away. It was like I was living on autopilot, day by day, just existing because I had to. But if I'd had the choice, if there was a way out that didn't involve hurting my family, I would have taken it. Sometimes, I wished I could just disappear completely. I remember watching a truck pass by one day, thinking I'd finally be free if it hit me right now. During one of our sessions, I spoke to Carol about all of this. I told her everything: the anxiety, the pressure, the way I felt trapped in a life I didn't want. I admitted to her that I felt like I was dying inside, little by little, every day. She listened quietly, then said, "You know what you need to do; you need to break off this engagement and go live your life. You need to go after your happiness."

I shook my head, tears filling my eyes. "I can't," I told her. I'm not strong enough to break an engagement. Do you know what that would do to my parents? The shame it would bring them. I can't do that to them again." "It's not shame, Nesrin. It's your life. You've been sacrificing your happiness for everyone else. But what about you? Don't you deserve to be happy, too?"

I wanted to believe her and follow her advice, but I couldn't. I told her, "It's not Malik's fault. He's a good man, but I know he'll never support my dream. He wants a wife who stays home, cooks, and cares for the children. He'd never accept me as a flight attendant, traveling the world. It's not his fault, and it's just how he sees life. And I'm stuck. My hands are tied."

Carol looked at me with so much empathy, but I could feel her frustration, too. She wanted me to fight for myself, to take that leap of faith. But I wasn't ready. Not yet. The pressure from everyone around me was too much, and I felt like I couldn't breathe. I was caught between the life I thought I had to live and the life I dreamed of, and the pain of being stuck in the middle was unbearable. Each day felt harder than the last. I was going to work, but without any will to be there. I would have done it if I could have stayed home, curled up in bed, and slept until my wedding day. I didn't want to stand up. I didn't want to eat. My body felt weak. My soul was tired. Everything in me was tired. I was simply existing, not living.

One morning, I saw a group of women standing by a donation stand on my way to work. They were collecting money for women with breast cancer. Something about them caught my attention, so I stopped. I only had 20 bucks with me, but I put it into the donation box. One of the women smiled at me and said, "Your hair is so beautiful. It's long and healthy."

Her words hit me. My hair had been falling out because of my depression, but it still looked good. She, on the other hand, had no hair at all. She was going through treatment for breast cancer, and her head was bare. Around the stand were pictures of other women wearing wigs, and something about those images made my heart ache. I felt bad for her, for all of them. I wanted to do something, anything, to help. That's when an idea hit me. Maybe I would feel better if I helped someone, even just a little. Without thinking twice, I ran into the first salon I saw. I stepped inside and said to the hairdresser, "Cut my hair. Cut it short."

The hairdresser tied my hair into a ponytail and snipped it off in one swift cut. When he handed it to me, my hair was just below my ears. I thanked him, put the ponytail into a bag, and rushed back to the stand. When I handed the bag to the lady who had complimented me earlier, she looked confused.

"What's this?" She asked, "It's my hair; you said it was pretty. I don't know if it's enough, but maybe you can make a wig out of it."

Her face softened as she opened the bag. Her eyes filled with tears as she looked at the hair. "We accept hair donations, but I didn't expect you to do this; real hair is expensive, and not everyone can afford a wig."

She hugged me tightly, and I could feel her gratitude. I told her, "Don't worry about me. Hair grows back. I just want you, or someone, to feel pretty, get back the confidence, and have the strength to go through the chemo treatments."

I left the stand feeling... conflicted. A part of me hoped this act of kindness would heal something inside me. That by helping someone else, I would feel whole again. But it didn't. I still felt broken. I walked away with short hair and a broken soul. When I arrived home that evening, my parents looked at me with wide eyes. They were shocked to see my hair so short. My mother was the first to speak.

"What happened? Are you okay? Is everything fine? Did you and Malik fight?" "No, there's nothing wrong between me and him. We're fine. I don't feel like myself anymore," I told her honestly.

They exchanged worried glances but didn't press further. They could tell something was off, but I wasn't ready to explain, and even if I did, I don't think they would have understood me. Later that night, Malik sent me a message. He had seen pictures of me with my new short hair and, unsurprisingly, was just as shocked as my parents, and he asked, "Why did you do that? You shouldn't have cut your hair. We're about to get married; brides in Lebanon should have long, beautiful hair so the hairdresser can style it properly. You've ruined that."

I stared at his message, feeling a surge of frustration. I didn't want to argue, but I couldn't let this go. I typed back, "I wasn't worried about my wedding day or my hair. I met a woman who needed it more than I did. She was battling cancer. Her self-esteem, her health, and her life—all of these are more important than my wedding hairstyle. She needed it, so I gave it to her."

"I loved your short hair, don't get me wrong, but you don't understand how this looks. People in Lebanon will talk about this. They'll say you're not a proper bride. It's not our tradition for brides to have short hair." I couldn't believe what I was reading. His words made me feel small, like my choice to help someone was a mistake simply because it didn't fit into his society's expectations.

"I don't care what people think; I did what I believed was right then. He was more worried about appearances and tradition than the meaning behind my actions. That wasn't the kind of support I wanted or needed. I sat there, staring at his messages, and wondered, if this was just about hair, how would he react to bigger decisions I might make? Decisions about my life, my dreams, or my future? We spent such a short time together that we didn't get to know each other properly, so there was a lot of his personality revealing itself to me slowly, and it started to bother me. I started to doubt marrying him, but it was already too late; I had no choice.

That night, we were all gathered around the dinner table. My mom had prepared Mloukhiyeh, a traditional Lebanese dish made with a plant similar to spinach, cooked with chicken and served with rice. Normally, this meal brought warmth and comfort, a time when the family would laugh and share stories. But that night, I could barely focus. I sat there quietly, picking at my food, barely tasting anything. My mom was excited as always, talking about the things she had bought for my honeymoon. She leaned toward me, smiling.

"I got you a few clothes for your honeymoon trip. You have to try them on later. I want to see how they look on you!" Her excitement was pure and genuine, but I couldn't match it. I looked down at my plate and mumbled, "It's fine. Just throw them in the bag. That's fine."

My voice was so low, so drained of energy, that the whole table grew quiet. My mom looked at me with concern. "Are you okay? We are worried about you; we don't know what's happening; we are trying to understand and help."

But before I could answer, something inside me shifted. A sudden heat rushed through my body, and I knew I was going to throw up. I jumped up from the table, barely managing to say, "Excuse me!" before running to the toilet. I didn't even make it to the toilet bowl, and I threw up in the sink. It came in waves, and it was so much that I couldn't stop. My body felt like it was rejecting everything, all the weight I had been carrying. My mom ran after me. She held my short hair back and stayed with me until it was over. When it finally stopped, I was trembling, and tears started streaming down my face. Then, suddenly, I exploded. I couldn't stop crying. I couldn't hold it in anymore. All the emotions I had been bottling up came pouring out of me. I cried uncontrollably, my body shaking as I gripped the edge of the sink. My mom wrapped her arms around me, holding me as tightly as she could, and she whispered close to my face, "Please, please talk to me. I'm here. Just tell me what's wrong."

But I couldn't. I didn't even know where to start. How could I explain everything I was feeling, the pressure, the pain, the way my soul felt like it was breaking apart? I just kept crying, screaming, and crying some more. It felt like something heavy was inside my chest, something I needed to get out, but I didn't know how. All I could do was cry. My mom didn't let go. She just held me, her own tears starting to fall. "It's okay, let it out. I'm here, I'm here."

At that moment, I wanted to tell her everything. I wanted to tell her that I wasn't okay, that I wasn't happy, that I didn't want the life I was preparing for. But I couldn't. I couldn't find the words, and the fear of disappointing her, of letting everyone down, was still too strong. After I had cried until no more tears were left, my mom helped me sit down. She brought me a glass of water, holding my hand tightly as though she feared I might fall apart again. Her face was full of worry. She didn't push me to talk anymore, but her silence spoke louder than any words. She guided me back to my bed, tucked me in like a child, and sat next to me for a long time. Her presence was comforting, but I couldn't shake the feeling that I was crumbling under the weight of a life I didn't want. A life that wasn't mine.

That night, as I lay in bed staring at the ceiling, I couldn't stop replaying everything in my mind. The wedding preparations, the pressure from my family, and Malik's disappointment over my short hair all felt suffocating. My body had screamed at me through the throwing up, the hair loss, and the anxiety, and I knew I couldn't ignore it any longer. I wasn't happy. I wasn't okay. The next day, I decided I needed to be honest with someone; if not my mom, then at least Carol, my therapist. During our session, I told her about the incident at dinner, the throwing up, and the way I felt like my body was shutting down. She listened carefully, her expression soft yet serious.

"Nesrin, your body is telling you what your heart already knows. You're not happy. This isn't the life you want. The question is, how much longer are you willing to live for others instead of yourself?"

Her words touched me because they were true. I was living to meet everyone else's expectations, my parents, Malik, and society's idea of what a bride should be. But what about me? Did I even have the courage to fight for myself, to fight for my dream?

"I'm scared," I admitted. "I'm scared of hurting everyone. I'm scared of disappointing my family again."

"Being scared is okay. It means you care. But being scared shouldn't stop you from living your truth. What's worse, hurting them for a little while or hurting yourself for the rest of your life?"

Her words stayed stuck with me long after the session ended. That evening, I sat alone in my room, staring at my reflection in the mirror. My short hair reminded me of a small moment of courage, something I had done for someone else to make them feel beautiful. Could I find that courage again, this time for myself? My head was like a fabric, working for 24 hours nonstop, full of doubts, insecurity, questions, and fear. That evening, while drowning in my thoughts, my phone beeped. I glanced at it, expecting another message from Malik about wedding plans or family traditions. But it wasn't from him. It was from Ziad. I hesitated before opening it, unsure if I wanted to hear what he had to say. When I finally read the message, my heart skipped a beat. He had sent me a link to an article. Dubai Airways was coming back to São Paulo to hire flight attendants.

"They're coming back. You have to go, Nesrin. You have to try again. Don't give up; don't get married. Follow your dreams. Fight for your dreams. I'll support you all the way." His words were passionate, filled with belief in me that I no longer had in myself. He didn't try to persuade me to choose him or leave Malik for him. He just wanted me to chase the dream I had buried, but I couldn't. I couldn't open that door again, only to be disappointed once more. I stared at the message for a long time, feeling the weight of his words pressing against the walls I had built around myself. Then, with shaky fingers, I replied, "Please, Ziad. Forget about me. Just forget. I'm not going. I'm not fighting for this anymore."

I sent the message, and it felt so wrong. Not because of him but because I knew I was lying to myself deep down. I wasn't just trying to convince him; I was trying to convince myself that I could let go of this dream. But could I? My phone stayed silent after that. Ziad didn't reply, and I sat there by my bed. The room felt smaller and suffocating. I told myself, looking at my reflection in the mirror, that it was for the best. For my own good. Better to settle into the life I was expected to live than to reopen old wounds by chasing something that had brought me so much pain. The days were slipping away, each one blurring into the next. Every morning, I would wake up feeling weaker than the day before. I had already lost 11 kilograms in just over 40 days since returning from Lebanon. My clothes no longer fit; they were all big, as if I was wearing an X-large garbage bag. And I barely recognized myself in the mirror.

My phone would buzz constantly with messages from my family in Lebanon. They were full of excitement, asking where the wedding would be, when the invitations would be sent, and what colors I had chosen for the theme. My cousins were thrilled, already planning their dresses, hairstyles, and makeup for the big day. Everyone around me was so invested in this new life of mine, so busy planning for the future I was supposed to have. Everyone except me. I didn't have the energy to join in their excitement. I didn't want to choose flowers or colors or even consider the wedding. I told my family to handle everything and make the decisions for me. Whatever they choose would be fine. I just didn't care. I couldn't care. My therapist, Carol, saw how much I was struggling.

During one of our sessions, she told me she would help me get a few days off work. She could see that I couldn't go anymore, not physically or emotionally. The thought of leaving the house, of seeing people, of putting on a fake smile was unbearable. She helped me file the necessary paperwork, and I was granted some time off due to my depression. For a while, I didn't have to go to work. But even with the days off, I didn't feel any better. I spent most of my time in bed, staring at the ceiling or sleeping.

The only thing I wanted was for time to pass quickly so the wedding would arrive and I wouldn't have to feel anything anymore. I avoided my phone as much as I could, ignoring the messages from my cousins, aunts, and uncles. Every notification felt like a reminder of how trapped I was. They were so happy and full of joy for me, and I didn't have the heart to tell them I wasn't happy. The life they were so excited about wasn't what I wanted. But I couldn't bring myself to disappoint them. So, I stayed quiet, letting them make the plans, while I sank deeper into depression and misery.

One morning, I woke up to the sound of my phone ringing. It was early, barely 6 a.m., and I felt groggy and confused as I reached for my phone. The caller ID read Ziad. I debated ignoring it for a moment, but something told me to answer. When I picked up, he said, "Look through your window."

Still half-asleep, I got up from bed and stumbled to the window. I pulled back the curtain and froze. There he was, standing outside my house.

"What are you doing here?" I hissed into the phone. "You're crazy! My dad's going to kill you. He hasn't forgiven you for everything that happened before, and my brothers can't wait to fill your face with more punches. Aren't you scared? They'll beat you up again if they see you! " He asked me to calm down with his usual soft voice, which always brought me peace, and asked me to come down and meet him by the front door because there was something very important he needed to discuss with me.

I hung up and ran downstairs, still in my pajamas, my hair unbrushed, and my face a mess. Depression had taken such a toll on me that I barely cared about how I looked anymore. When I opened the door, I whispered my frustration at him, asking him what he was doing there, trying to keep my voice low so my family wouldn't hear, and he said

"Today is the Dubai Airways assessment day. I came to take you there." I stared at him in disbelief, stood firmly in front of him, and said, with an angry voice, "I'm not going, and you know you can't just show up to the assessment day. You have to go to the open day first. Besides, I'm engaged. I'm getting married. I can't just throw everything in the air and go."

He didn't back down. "I already spoke to the Dubai Airways third party who conducts the open day; they know you. You've attended so many times that they didn't need you to attend an open day. They said you could jump straight to the assessment, and with the help of your brother Walid, we registered you. They're expecting you today."

I grabbed my hair with my two hands and felt like pulling it out of frustration, and I told him, "I told you; I'm not going. My parents would never allow it, and my fiancé would never allow it. I'm not going. You need to stop this madness."

Just as I said those words, I heard a voice behind me. "Yes, you are going."

I turned around and saw my dad standing behind me and my mother beside him. My heart stopped. "What?" I asked, completely stunned. He looked me in the eyes with a calm but serious expression. You are going this time; we're letting you go. You'll go to the interview. This is what you want, what you have always wanted. You have our blessing and permission to go."

I couldn't believe what I was hearing. My father, the man who had always been scared of me losing myself to this scary world, was always so protective. He always dreamt of seeing me marry, build a family, and be a respectful housewife, and he gave me his blessing. My head was spinning. I thought I was dreaming for a second, but it was all reality this time. I felt a flicker of hope for the first time in what felt like forever. But I was also terrified. I looked at both of my parents and said, "But what if I fail again? It will be my 5th failure. I'm so scared of disappointing myself and you." My parents had their eyes wide open and stared at each other with their mouths open, too, and Dad said, "It will be the 5th time. When did you go on the 4th?

I didn't know where to hide my face; I told him it was a long story, and for the sake of my mental health and his mental health as well, it was better if we didn't go into details. Then I remembered that I didn't have anything ready. I told them I couldn't just go like this. I needed time to fix my makeup, and my hair was short; I didn't know if I could fix it properly for the interview. I couldn't show up there looking unpresentable, and I would be eliminated straight away. Then my mom, with a very smiley face, said, "Don't worry. I have provided everything, and everything is under control."

Then I saw a car speeding over. My hairdresser, Jill, and Chris brought inside a huge bag with everything they needed to fix my hair and makeup.

Chris joked, "Listen, lady, you better make it happen this time. If I have to wake up this early again, it better be because you're living with a view of the Burj Khalifa."

Am I dreaming? I asked them. Is this all real? Are we really doing this? My eyes were full of tears, but this time, they were happy tears I hadn't had in so long. I almost forgot how it feels to have a mixed feeling, to have the soul alive and the eyes sparkling. My mom looked at me and said, "I shouldn't have let happen to you what happened to me. I didn't have a choice. I wasn't brave enough to raise my voice when I was your age, but you were; you shouted loud about what makes you happy, and I should have listened. I'm so sorry I didn't listen earlier. So now go get ready and make our dream come true."

I hugged her so hard, telling her that I loved her and would make her proud. Then I looked at my dad and asked him, "But Dad, what will people say?"

Dad answered me, "They will say... lucky daughter of his, she gets to travel the whole world."

I hugged him, too, with my eyes filled with tears. I looked back to Ziad and told him, "Thank you," with only the movement of my lips. Then I ran upstairs because the girls were waiting to turn me into a flight attendant.

I was finally ready to go to the interview. Walking down the stairs, I heard Ziad chatting in the living room with my parents. He was telling them about how he had broken up with his girlfriend, how things hadn't worked out between them, and how his parents hadn't accepted her. My parents were listening attentively, sipping Arabic coffee, and surprisingly, they were actually having a good conversation. Ziad seemed to be in my parents' good graces for the first time in months. I reached the bottom of the stairs, feeling a surge of confidence.

I had taken my time to prepare. My makeup was flawless, my short hair styled neatly, and my outfit was everything a flight attendant should look like. I wore black stockings with a knee-length skirt, a crisp white shirt under a blazer, and high heels that clicked with purpose as I stepped. I looked like I belonged to the skies. I stood in the doorway of the living room, catching their attention. "I'm ready," I said simply. Ziad looked up at me, his face lighting up with pride. But before we could leave, I heard footsteps behind me. I turned to see Walid, my older brother, coming down the stairs, wearing a black tuxedo with his beard shaved.

"I'm ready, too," said Walid.

I stopped staring at him, confused. Where are you going?" I asked.

"With you to the interview, I registered and was accepted to attend the assessment day," he replied.

I stared at him, horrified, saying, "No. No, no, no, no, no, no, no," shaking my head and pointing my finger at him. I continued mumbling, "I've seen this movie before, Walid. I bring someone with me, and that person passes, and I don't. I'm not doing that again."

With a sincere and firm tone, Walid replied, "Come on, you always say that what's meant to be yours will be yours. Whether I go or don't go, if it's meant to be yours, it will be; I won't take that away from you."

I crossed my arms, still staring angrily at him: "Walid, I'm serious. You're not coming with me."

But before I could argue further, my father spoke up from the living room, "Let him go, and he just wants to try. Besides, you've already tried so many times. What's the harm?"

I opened my mouth to protest, but no words came out. My father's words cut deeper than he probably realized. It was true; I had tried so many times and failed. Maybe I was scared. Scared that if Walid came along and succeeded and I didn't, it would confirm all my doubts about myself. But wasn't Ziad right when he said I needed to fight for my dream? And wasn't Walid right, too? If this were meant to be mine, it would be mine, no matter what.

"Fine, but don't expect me to be nice if you pass and I don't."

Walid laughed, throwing an arm around my shoulder "Deal, now let's go. We've got a flight to catch."

Walid and I arrived at the interview location. Ziad dropped us off at the front of the hotel and said he would sit at a coffee shop nearby and wait for us. His calm energy was comforting, and I nodded before walking inside with my brother. The atmosphere was different this time. Unlike the open days in the past, which were always crowded with hundreds of dreamers, this was the assessment day, and only about 85 people were there. These were the candidates Dubai Airways believed had the potential to become flight attendants. I reminded myself of how far I'd come to make it to this room.

The process began with us being divided into groups. We were asked to sit in circles, and the dynamic was slightly different this time. Each person was asked to stand up and talk about their favorite movie and explain why it was their favorite. My turn came, and I realized something felt different as I stood up. I wasn't scared. My heart wasn't pounding, my hands weren't shaking, and my breath was steady. For the first time, I felt calm, confident, and ready. Maybe it was because I had my parents' blessing this time, or maybe my brother was by my side, and Ziad was waiting just outside, rooting for me.

Their energy surrounded me, lifting me in a way I hadn't felt before. I stood tall, looking into the eyes of every candidate and interviewer in the room:

"My favorite movie is Desert Flower," I began. "It's a true story about a Somali teenager named Waris Dirie, living in the desert as part of a tribe. She had to follow the rules and traditions of her culture, even though she didn't believe in them. One day, she managed to escape the tribe and traveled to London in search of a better life. She started at the very bottom, working as a cleaner, wiping floors, and getting humiliated by everyone. She didn't have a home and slept in bathrooms to survive. But then, one day, someone noticed her, saw her potential, and gave her a chance to do a photo shoot. From that moment, her life changed. She became a model, and her face was featured in magazines around the world. How she fought for her freedom and transformed her life through courage and persistence inspires me. That's why Desert Flower is my favorite movie."

When I finished, I sat back down and could feel the room's energy shift. The interviewers nodded, scribbling notes, and I felt a small sense of accomplishment. I had spoken from the heart. After everyone had their turn, the interviewers handed us envelopes. "These will let you know if you've passed to the next stage," they announced. My hands trembled as I held the envelope, afraid to open it. "Oh my God, should I open it?" I whispered to Walid.

"Open it," he said, without any patience. "What are you waiting for?"

I took a deep breath and tore it open. Inside were the words I had been waiting for, "Congratulations, you have passed to the next step of this interview." Relief washed over me, but I knew it wasn't over yet. A lot of people didn't make it and were sent home. But Walid and I made it to the next stage, "the English test."

We were seated at desks and handed three-page tests. The questions were about grammar, fill-in-the-blanks, and writing an essay. It wasn't easy, but it wasn't overly difficult either. I had studied and prepared for this for the past 4 years, and Walid and I both had strong English skills. We handed in our papers and waited for the results when we finished. Another envelope. My nerves were on edge again, but when I opened it, the words inside filled me with joy: "Congratulations, you have passed to the next stage." I couldn't believe it. Walid and I exchanged a look of disbelief. "We made it to the final stage of the assessment day. I'm hyperventilating, and I can't lose my composure. I said to Walid with my voice and eyes filled with hope.

The final stage was the hardest yet. Only about 25 of us were left and placed into smaller groups. Each group was given a scenario to solve, with the interviewers playing the role of clients. The goal was to work together to find a solution to a customer service problem. They wanted to see how we communicated, handled pressure, and worked as a team.

Thanks to all the blogs and articles I had read about flight attendant interviews, I knew how to approach it. I shared my ideas confidently but made sure to include my teammates. "What do you think?" I would ask after suggesting a solution, showing that I valued everyone's input. Our group worked well together, and when the activity ended, I felt proud of how we had performed. The final envelope came, and this one held the most weight. It determined who would make it to the final interview. I held it in my hands, my heart pounding, and opened it slowly. My eyes scanned the words, and when I saw, "Congratulations, you have passed to the final interview." I couldn't contain my emotions. I turned to Walid, who was grinning from ear to ear. We had both made it.

Only 15 people were left from the original 85, and I was one of them. I couldn't believe it. I had passed all the stages and reached the final interview, which would take place the next day. I felt like my dream was within reach for the first time in years. It was time to go home and start getting ready for the judgment day, the final interview.

CHAPTER 19

Judgment Day

يوم الحساب

I t was the day of the final interview, or my Judgment Day, as I always called it. I woke up early, my nerves jumping and my heart beating like a hammer hitting a wall. Today, I would sit face-to-face with the interviewer in a private room. It would just be the two of us. She would ask me questions, and I would have to answer with poise and confidence, showing her why I deserved to wear the Dubai Airways uniform. I got out of bed, my heart racing, and began getting ready. Every detail mattered today. My makeup needed to be flawless, my outfit sharp, and my energy calm but professional. This was my moment, and I couldn't afford to let nerves get the better of me.

As I was getting ready, I heard the sound of a motorcycle outside the house, followed by the beep of its horn. I was so confused; it was very early for someone to be visiting. I wasn't expecting anything or anyone. Curious, I ran downstairs to see what it was; it was a delivery; of course, the first thing that came to my mind was, "What had Ziad planned this time?" The delivery driver handed me a small box. I brought the box inside, carefully opening it to find a small note on top. The handwriting was familiar, and my heart swelled with emotion as I read the words. "This was my lucky lipstick for years, and now I want it to be your lucky lipstick as well. Wear this for your interview for good luck and have faith."

She had signed the note at the bottom, "The Jewish therapist who loves you and wishes you all the happiness this universe can give you."

It was from Carol, my therapist. I sat there holding the note and the lipstick, tears filling my eyes. Carol had been with me through every moment of my struggle. She knew my pain, my doubts, and my fears, and yet she had always believed in me. She passed that belief on to me through this small but powerful gift. I looked at the lipstick in my hand. It was a deep, confident shade of red and seemed to hold a certain kind of magic. At that moment, I promised myself that I would wear this lipstick and carry Carol's faith with me into that interview.

Whatever happened today, I wouldn't let fear win; I continued getting ready, taking my time to ensure every detail was perfect. My makeup was flawless, my hair was neatly styled, and, of course, I wore Carol's lucky red lipstick. It was bold and beautiful, and as I looked in the mirror, I felt a wave of confidence wash over me. For the first time in a long time, I thought to myself, I look pretty. I feel confident. I can do this. While waiting for Walid to get ready, I practiced in front of the mirror. I rehearsed how I would introduce myself, how I would smile, and how I would answer the questions with calm and clarity. I watched my posture and my expressions and tried to imagine the interview going perfectly.

Soon, we arrived at the interview venue. Walid and I sat in the corridor outside the interview rooms, waiting for our turns. The air was tense; everyone there knew what was at stake. Walid was called in before me, and as he disappeared behind the door, I was left alone with my thoughts. My leg started shaking uncontrollably. I tapped my foot against the floor, trying to ease the anxiety building up inside me. My hands were sweaty, and

I felt my heart beating faster with each passing moment. This is a big step, I thought to myself. It wasn't just about the interview but about everything this moment represented. I kept repeating small instructions to myself in my mind, like a mantra. Look the interviewer in the eye. Don't look down. Answer naturally. Smile. Stay calm. But the nervousness still lived inside of me. Then, I remembered something.

I reached into my purse and pulled out a small, folded piece of paper. It was old, the edges slightly worn, but it was one of my most treasured possessions. It was a handwritten prayer, "Ayatul Kursi." Given to me by my cousin Rayan before we parted. She had written it for me years ago, telling me it was one of the most powerful verses in the Quran. She said it would protect me, open doors, and ease the weight in my heart whenever I felt scared or uncertain. I unfolded the paper and quietly read the words to myself, letting the prayer fill me with a sense of peace and strength.

"Allah—there is no God except Him, the Ever-Living, the Sustainer of all existence. Neither drowsiness overtakes Him nor sleep. To Him belongs whatever is in the heavens and whatever is on the earth. Who is it that can intercede with Him except by His permission? He knows what is presently before them and what will be after them, and they encompass not a thing of His knowledge except for what He wills. His Kursi extends over the heavens and the earth, and their preservation tires Him not. And He is the Highest, the Greatest."

I tucked the paper back into my purse and deeply breathed as I finished reading. I could feel a small shift inside me. The nerves were still there, but they were no longer overwhelming. I closed my eyes briefly and whispered, inshallah, reminding myself that whatever was meant to happen would happen. It was my turn to go inside. Walid was still with his interviewer, so I took a deep breath, stood up, and walked toward the door. My heart was racing, but I reminded myself to stay composed. I opened the door, stepped in, and greeted the interviewer with a firm handshake. "Good morning," I said, introducing myself with a smile. She gestured for me to sit down, and as I took my seat, I noticed my CV and photos neatly arranged on the table in front of her. She flipped through the papers for a moment before looking up at me.

"You've quite an interesting background," she began. "You speak four languages. How did that happen?" "I grew up in Colombia, so Spanish was the first additional language I learned. Later, we moved to Lebanon to reconnect with our roots, where I learned Arabic and embraced the culture. English came from my education in Lebanon, and I picked up Portuguese over the past four years, living and working here in Brazil."

She nodded, impressed. "That's fascinating," she said. - "Now, I will ask you a few situational questions. Take your time to think before answering." I nodded, folding my hands in my lap and hiding them under the table so she wouldn't see me trembling. "How are you feeling?" she asked. "Nervous," I admitted with a small laugh. "But I think that's only natural. I've wanted this for so long, so it's impossible not to feel a little overwhelmed."

She smiled gently. "It's okay to feel that way. Let's begin."

Question 1: Have you ever done something to demonstrate respect toward someone else's religion or culture? "Yes," I said confidently, "One example is my relationship with Carol. She's Jewish, and I'm Muslim, but we have always supported each other despite our different beliefs. We don't let politics, war, or anything else interfere with our shared connection. In fact, (I continued, gesturing toward my lips) She's the one who gave me this red lipstick to wear today. She said it was her lucky lipstick and wanted it to be mine. To me, that symbolizes not just respect but love and understanding. We are proof that a Muslim and a Jew can share a space, respect each other, and care for each other deeply."

Question 2: Have you ever gone out of your way to protect or help someone at work?

I paused briefly, then shared another story.

"Yes, at the current law firm where I work now, there was a day when a document went missing, and my colleagues were at risk of losing their jobs. I knew their families depended on them, so I took the blame. I was still on probation and didn't know if I would pass the probation. It was a risk for me, but I couldn't stand the thought of them getting hurt; they had more to lose than me. Ultimately, I managed to save them from big trouble and learned how important it is not always to put ourselves first. It's okay to go our way to save someone's day." The interviewer made a note on her paper and smiled. "That's a great example of teamwork and compassion," she said.

Question 3: Have you ever had a conflict with a coworker? How did you resolve it?

This question brought Tamara to mind instantly. I took a deep breath before answering.

"Yes, I have; I worked with a colleague who made a disrespectful comment about my religion. It was difficult, but I chose not to engage in an argument. Instead, I handled it professionally by reporting the incident to management. The issue was resolved, and I think it was an example of how important it is to remain calm and mature in conflict situations." I didn't mention that Tamara was fired, but I could tell the interviewer appreciated how I framed my response. "

As the interview went on, it felt like she asked me about everything I had lived through in the past few years: every challenge, lesson, and hardship. And because those experiences were real, the words came naturally. I didn't have to fake anything or try too hard. I just shared the truth. When the interview ended, she stood up, shook my hand, and said, "Thank you for your time. You've given us a lot to think about."

I stepped out of the room, feeling a strange mix of relief and nervousness. Walid was outside waiting for me. He asked me how it had gone, and I told him it felt so natural, as if I was telling her the story of my life. The questions she asked matched each event that has happened to me; I wondered if it was destiny, if it was God's plan, not to let me pass all the other times because all those things needed to happen to me for me to be able to answer the final interview questions and get the job. Walid told me it was possible and that God's plan never failed. Sometimes, we wonder why bad things happen to us, and most of the time, they happen for our own good, but we just realize it after the storm is gone.

There was nothing left to do but wait. The hardest part of the process was over, and now it was out of my hands. All I could do was hope and pray for the best. I knew the waiting wouldn't be easy. Talita had told me it took her about three weeks to get her final approval. So, I tried to prepare myself for the long days ahead. The 14 other candidates and I decided to create a Facebook group to stay connected. It became our lifeline, a space where we could share updates, encourage one another, and ease some tension. Every day, someone would post a message, "Any news?" or "Has anyone heard anything yet?" We were all in the same boat, anxiously waiting for our futures to be decided.

Dubai Airways also gave us usernames and passwords to access their online portal. This was where we could check the status of our applications and track the progress of the recruitment process. I quickly became obsessed with it. I log in multiple times a day, refreshing the page over and over again, hoping to see some change in my status. The application statuses were cryptic, with vague updates like "Application under review" or "Interview in progress." But sometimes, the status would change before an official call came, and that was what kept me glued to the portal. I wanted to be the first to know if something changed, even if it was just a small update. I also kept in constant communication with the other candidates. We became a little community united by the same dream. Every day, we shared our thoughts, anxieties, and excitement. Some of them were confident, saying, "We've got this! They wouldn't have taken us this far if they didn't see potential." Others were more nervous, doubting themselves and second-guessing their answers from the interview. I was somewhere in between. One moment, I felt hopeful, and the next, I was filled with self-doubt. I would log into the portal late at night, staring at the same words, refreshing the page as if waiting for a sign. My heart would race every time the page loaded, even though nothing had changed. It was exhausting but impossible to stop.

I lived my days and continued life as if nothing had changed. I went to work, acted normal, and didn't tell anyone about reaching the final stage of the Dubai Airways interview or even that I had applied. I didn't want anyone to ruin it for me like Tamara once did. I loved the girls, and I trusted them with all my heart, but I also once trusted Tamara, and she stabbed me in my back. I couldn't risk it anymore. To my colleagues, I was still the bride-to-be, planning her wedding. They would ask me questions about the wedding colors, the venue, and the honeymoon, and I would smile and give them vague answers. Inside, I knew the truth: there was no wedding planned. I hadn't touched anything related to it. But I couldn't keep it hidden forever. I decided I needed to be honest with Malik. One evening, I called him, feeling the weight of the conversation before it even began. I told him, "I need to tell you something; when I was in Lebanon, I went behind your back and applied for the Dubai Airways interview. I didn't pass then, but I just wanted you to know the truth."

Silence was on the other end of the phone for a long moment. Then he spoke, his voice disappointed, "How could you do that, Nesrin? I've been honest with you from the beginning. I thought we were a couple. I thought we were supposed to trust each other."

"I'm sorry, I didn't know how to tell you. I didn't want to disappoint you or anyone else, and back then, I had doubts about getting married and big hopes for a future as a flight attendant." "You didn't just disappoint me," he said sharply. "You betrayed my trust. I asked for your hand in marriage because I wanted a wife. Someone who would build a home with me and be by my side. Not a... not a waiter in the sky."

He was so rude, but I wasn't surprised. I would expect this kind of reaction from him or any other man from that village. I had always known how he felt about my dream. Still, hearing it out loud hurt more than I had expected. "I understand your frustration, Malik. You were always fully committed to us and our future, and I struck you with this news. But I also need to tell you that I applied again here in Brazil for the flight attendant role. I've reached the final stage of the interview, and I'm waiting to hear back from them."

Malik's disappointment turned into something colder. I could feel the weight of his words before he spoke. His tone changed completely to a selfish tone filled with anger, disgust, and frustration. "Then you've already made your choice, Nesrin. You've chosen your dream over us. You've chosen to live a life that I can't accept. This engagement isn't going to work, Nesrin. I can't trust you anymore, and I can't accept the life you choose, lies, and betrayal."

Tears filled my eyes, but I didn't fight him. I knew he was right. This wasn't the wife he had always wanted, and I couldn't be what he always wanted, fully committed to a husband, house, and family. I had feelings for him, and we shared good memories in Lebanon, but I couldn't give him what he dreamt about: "a family." Slowly, I slipped the engagement ring off my finger, feeling the cool metal slide away. I placed it in the drawer beside my bed, knowing our chapter had ended. I felt a strange sense of relief for the first time in weeks. The weight of the ring was gone, and so was the weight of pretending to be someone I wasn't. I didn't care about what people would say or invent about me. I knew I would be the latest news in my village and maybe the entire countryside region. I knew how they would picture me, the lies they would tell, and the things I would be called, but I didn't care. All I cared about was me, putting myself first, and my happiness above all. I had finally understood what Carol meant all this time, about starting to take care of myself and live for me, not for others. It felt so good to be the owner of my own story, the author of my own book, without letting anyone hold the pen on my behalf and write something I wouldn't like.

A few weeks had passed, and the waiting game had only gotten harder. Some of the candidates from our group began receiving what we called "the golden call." The golden call was when HR from Dubai Airways would call to tell you the words every aspiring flight attendant wanted to hear, "You're hired." The news began trickling into our Facebook group. One by one, people posted their excitement, sharing screenshots or updates saying they'd received the call. Everyone congratulated them, but with every post, my anxiety grew. I couldn't help but wonder, "Why haven't I heard anything yet?"

Not everyone was getting good news, though. Alongside the celebrations were posts from candidates who had received rejection emails. They would write, "I didn't pass the final interview, but I'll try again in a few months." Seeing those messages only made me more nervous. Whenever my phone rang, my heart would jump, hoping it was the golden call. But it never was. My parents started asking about the results more frequently. They had seen how much I had suffered and how much I had fought to get this far. I could feel how badly they wanted me to succeed, to see me finally happy. They were even more anxious than I was, especially since Walid and I hadn't heard anything yet. My mom would ask me every morning,

"Have you heard anything? Did they call?" and I'd shake my head and say, "Not yet." Even people outside my family were asking. Jill and Chris at the salon asked me every time I stopped by. "Did you get the call?" "Are we waking up in Dubai next week?" they'd say with excited smiles. Each time, I'd have to explain that a few candidates had been hired, but I hadn't heard anything yet. Even my therapist, Carol, kept asking me during our sessions. She wanted me so badly to succeed. The more time passed, the more nervous I became. I started obsessively checking the Dubai Airways portal, refreshing it repeatedly to see if there were any changes to my application status. There were none. I tried to stay calm, but the anxiety was getting worse. Whenever I opened the Facebook group and saw another golden call post, my heart ached a little more. I wanted so badly to be one of them. I kept reminding myself of everything I had gone through to get to this point, of how much I had fought for this dream. But the waiting was unbearable. I felt like my entire future was balancing on a knife's edge, and all I could do was hope for the best. The waiting was playing with my nerves. Each passing day without an answer from Dubai Airways added to my anxiety and stress. I was losing sleep, obsessing over every little detail, and feeling like a house of cards; one little blow and I would break. One afternoon, I was at Jill's, the neighborhood salon. As I sat there, letting her work on my hair, she looked at me with kindness in her eyes and said,"

"I'm going to give you a gift you can't refuse." I raised an eyebrow, curious. "What kind of gift?" "A prayer, Nesrin. The most beautiful gift someone can receive is a prayer. It's pure, and it shows that someone cares about you. That's the truest proof of love and caring."

Her words felt like angels singing in my ears. She was a person with a good heart and a sparkling soul. You could tell she would always wish me well and never ill. Someone who would only want to see others happy without any envy. Someone who would do good without expecting anything in return. I accepted her beautiful prayers. Even though we were from different religions, I was happy she was willing to pray for me in her ways and what she believed in.

Jill asked me to write my full name, my mother's name, and my date of birth on a piece of paper. She said she was going to organize a special prayer day for me. She would take my information to her church and pray for me the next day. As we talked, Chris overheard our conversation and joined in. She told me she would pray for me as well; at the same time, Jill was praying. Chris, being Buddhist, said she would pray in her way, in her temple. I was overwhelmed by their kindness. Later, during my therapy session with Carol, I shared what Jill and Chris planned to do. Carol listened quietly, smiled, and said, "I will pray for you too. In Judaism, if you are okay with that."

I laughed and told her that if she had asked me this question 5 years ago, my answer would have been a big no, and I would have blocked her number, but I was a better person thanks to her. I learned how to love people despite what they choose to believe or follow. Learned to stop judging and assume that all our fingers are the same. She held my hand and said, "Yes, it doesn't matter what religion we follow. What matters is that we believe in what we're doing. Prayers are universal. They're an act of love. And I want to do this for you."

I felt a wave of warmth and gratitude wash over me. Everything they were doing, even a simple prayer, felt so powerful and big. A gift that wasn't materialistic or about money or appearances. A gift that would come from the heart and soul. I felt so blessed for the first time in a very long time.

When I got home that evening, I shared everything with my parents. I told them about the ladies at the salon and Carol. My mom's eyes lit up, and she immediately said, "We'll pray too. And we'll call Aunt Fatima. We'll all pray together tomorrow."

The plan was set. The next day, at 7 p.m., everyone would pray for me in their way. Jill would pray in her church. Chris would pray in her temple. Carol would pray in Judaism. And my family, along with Aunt Fatima, would pray in Islam. Each one, in their own home or place of worship, would offer their prayers at the same time. The next day, as the clock struck 7 p.m., I couldn't help but feel the energy surrounding me. Though I was alone in my room, I imagined Jill at her church, Chris in her temple, Carol in her synagogue, and my family bending their knees on the prayer mat at home. Each one is praying for me, sending their love and hope to God and the universe for my dream to come true. It didn't matter to me that they came from different religions. What mattered was that they cared enough to take time out of their day to think of me, to send their prayers and wishes into the world. It was humbling, and I felt a sense of peace for the first time in weeks. As the prayers ended, I whispered my own silent "Inshallah." I didn't know the future, but I felt surrounded by love at that moment.

That night, after all the prayers had been performed and the day's emotions had settled, I went to bed. My mind was quieter than it had been in weeks, though the anxiety was still playing a bit around my body; as I drifted off to sleep, I hoped for peace, even if just for a few hours. And then I had the dream; my great-grandmother appeared again, just as she had before. She looked radiant, sitting in a chair with a calm and regal presence. She was dressed in white, her hijab perfectly framing her serene face. There was a lightness around her, almost as if she was glowing. In the dream, I was on my knees in front of her, my hands resting on her knees. I was crying deep, heavy sobs. My whole body shook as I begged her, "Please, please, open the doors for me. Please, make it come true. I need it. I need this."

She reached down and gently placed her hands over mine. Her touch was warm and comforting, and it felt like all the love in the world was pouring into me through her hands. I could feel her touch. I could feel her hands. It was so real. Then she spoke, her voice soft and sweet, filled with an undeniable sense of certainty: "The doors are already open; they always have been open."

Her words comforted me in the dream; she said the words my ears craved. The tears stopped falling down my face, and I looked up at her, confused but comforted. She smiled at me, a smile so full of love and reassurance that it erased all my fears in that moment. I woke up suddenly, and the dream was still vivid. I sat in bed, trying to catch my breath, my heart racing. Her words replayed in my head, "The doors are already open. They always have been open." I didn't know exactly what she meant, but I felt a strange sense of calm. It was as if she was telling me that everything was already in motion, that the outcome was already written. I didn't need to beg or plead anymore. All I needed to do was trust. I googled what tears meant in dreams, and the result was the Arabic word "Fajar," which translates to "happiness and open doors" in English. I tried to go back to sleep after the dream, but my mind was spinning with my great-grandmother's words, "The doors are already open. They always have been open."

Was it a sign? Or was it just my subconscious trying to calm me down? I didn't know, but the peace I had felt during the dream was breathtaking, giving me a sense of quiet hope. Eventually, exhaustion pulled me back to sleep. Then, suddenly, my phone rang. My phone's sound, set at full volume, woke me up. My heart skipped a beat as I reached for the phone, the screen lighting up in the dark room. The number was unfamiliar, but the country code, "+971," caught my attention. I froze before picking it up; it was a Dubai number.

Hands trembling, I answered. "Hello?" There was a pause, then a voice on the other end. "Nesrin? Nesrin?" The voice was professional but warm. "Yes, it's me, Nesrin." Congratulations, dear, you have been hired to work for Dubai Airways." Time seemed to stop. I sat there, frozen, clutching the phone to my ear as the words sank in. I couldn't speak, couldn't breathe. I felt a rush of emotions: relief, disbelief, and joy.

The voice continued, explaining the next steps, the formalities, and the timeline for my relocation. But I barely heard the details. All I could think was, It's real. It's happening. I did it. When the call ended, I sat there silently, holding the phone. My great-grandmother's words echoed in my mind again, "The doors are already open." She was right. They had been open all along; I just needed to wait for my time to come, and like my uncle, Othman, said to me once, "Don't rush the river; it runs by itself." And I kept trying to rush things instead of letting it happen at its own timing.

I stood up, still in disbelief, and walked to my parents' room. Gently, I knocked on their door. My mom opened it; her eyes were heavy with sleep, but the moment she saw my face, she already knew I had been hired, and we both started to scream, hug, and cry because we had made our dream come true. I did it for her, and I did it for me. Dad joined us, groggy but smiling, as my mom repeated the news to him. "She did it. She got the job." Tears filled my eyes. I jumped into their bed and hugged them both. After everything, the rejection, the heartbreak, and the sacrifices, I finally made it.

I had fought for my dream, and now it was real. After that, I ran to get my phone, and I called Paulina. In the middle of the night, I woke her up and scared her; she thought someone had died or a terrible thing had happened, and I only said to her, "I made it, and I'm going home." She already knew what I meant. I could feel the joy and the happiness in her voice. She said she always knew I was going to make it. I lay back down. For the first time in weeks, I felt a glimmer of hope. It could be the power of the prayers, or maybe it was my hard work all this time or a mix of everything that made this dream possible. And I just needed to believe in the process.

CHAPTER 20

Independence Day

عيد الاستقلال

The next morning, the weight of my dream finally coming true felt lighter and more real. The first thing I did was pick up my phone and call Ziad. When he answered, I couldn't help but break the news to him straight away without going into circles and endless boring conversations: "I made it; I passed. Dubai Airways officially hired me. And if I died and came back to life a hundred times and thanked you every time I was re-born, I don't think it would still be enough."

There was a pause, and then I heard his voice light up with joy. With his tone filled with pride, he said, "I knew it, I knew you could do it, Nesrin. That's why I didn't let you give up. I believed in you, even when you didn't believe in yourself and had given up on everything."

His words touched me deeply. Ziad had been a constant source of encouragement, even when I felt like giving up. He reminded me of the strength I had buried under fear and self-doubt, and now here I was, standing on the edge of a new life, thanks to him. If it weren't for him fighting and pressuring me, I wouldn't have made it come true, and I told him that on the phone. I would carry him in my heart forever, until I grow old, until my last breath. Later that day, I went to work, a place that had been my home for the past four years. The faces, routines, and desks I had sat at for so long now felt different. This was the last time I would walk through those doors as an employee. I went straight to my manager to share the news, unable to hold back my smile, "Dubai Airways has hired me. I'll need to give my resignation."

My manager's face lit up with surprise and pride, and they said, "You're leaving us for something incredible. Congratulations, you deserve this."

Afterward, I sat at my desk for one last task, writing my farewell email. I thought of Thalia, how she had done the same thing before leaving for Dubai, and now it was my turn. The words came naturally, pouring out of my heart as I reflected on the journey that had brought me to this moment. I wrote:

Dear Team,

Today, I am writing to say goodbye and thank you. These past four years have been some of the most transformative years of my life. I joined this company as a girl, and I'm leaving as a woman. I want to thank each of you for shaping who I am today. When I came to Brazil, I was just an innocent Arabic girl, a village girl who didn't know much about life. But you took me under your wing. You taught me how to write emails, how to behave professionally, and how to speak Portuguese. You taught me how to navigate this world with confidence and grace. You have changed me completely inside out. If I pass the Dubai Airways interview and if I'm about to live my dream, it's because of all of you. You trained, guided, supported, and made me believe in myself. I will never forget what you've done for me. Of course, we had our ups and downs, but I cherish the positive days, which are way more than the negative. Thank you for being my family here, giving me strength, and helping me grow professionally and personally.

This isn't goodbye; it's a see you later. With love and gratitude, The Arabic girl.

I read the email one last time before sending it to the team. My hands trembled as I hit Send. Moments later, my inbox began filling with replies, each kind and supportive. Some congratulated me, others said they would miss me terribly, and a few told me how proud they were of my accomplishments. As soon as my farewell email was sent, the girls began pouring onto my floor, their faces full of warmth and emotion. They came to hug me, say goodbye, and wish me luck. Their words and gestures made me realize just how much I had been a part of this place and how much this place had been a part of me.

I hugged each of them, thanking them for everything, holding back my tears. Finally, it was time to go. I took the elevator down, my heart heavy yet full. I returned my company ID and signed the resignation paperwork with a steady hand. It felt official now; my chapter at the law firm had ended. As I left the building, I turned around to take it all in one last time. The sleek, pretty exterior of the building had been my workplace for the past four years. A place where I had laughed, cried, struggled, and grown.

I couldn't help but remember that very first day, the day I arrived late for the interview. My hair was a mess, and my self-esteem was at its lowest. I had walked in that day thinking I wouldn't get the job, that I wasn't good enough. But I did get it. And that moment had marked the beginning of a transformation I didn't even realize I needed. I stood there for a moment, letting the memories wash over me. The laughter I had shared with my colleagues, the lessons I had learned, and even the challenges that had shaped me into who I am now. I whispered a quiet "thank you to the building," to the people inside it, and to the experiences that had prepared me for the next chapter of my life. With one last look, I turned and walked away, feeling lighter with every step. I left that building with open doors, on good terms, and deeply grateful. This wasn't an ending; it was a new beginning.

My mom and I sat on the bedroom floor, surrounded by an explosion of clothes, shoes, and bags. She was helping me pack for my move to Dubai, and it felt surreal. Just weeks ago, I had been packing for a completely different future, a life as a bride, a wife, someone who was about to settle down. The bag I had prepared for my wedding was still in the corner of the room, filled with delicate outfits, accessories, and items for a life I was no longer pursuing. My mom laughed as we started unpacking it together.

"We're trading the wife life for the Dubai life," she joked, holding up a pair of silk slippers she had bought for my honeymoon. I laughed with her, the reality of the moment sinking in. "I guess we are," I said. "It's crazy how life changes, isn't it?"

One by one, we replaced the items meant for my wedding with things I would need for my new life as a flight attendant. I need practical clothes, comfortable shoes, a travel diary, and small keepsakes to remind me of my home. It felt like shedding old skin, leaving behind a version of myself that no longer existed. Even my dad joined in to help with the packing. He wasn't the type to get involved in things like this, but seeing the sheer amount of stuff I had to organize, he rolled up his sleeves and got to work. My mom handed him things to pack while he tried to fit everything into the bags, muttering under his breath about how I would exceed the luggage weight limit.

"Why do you need all these books, Nesrin? Your bags will be overweight," said Baba. "Baba, these are non-negotiable. I don't go anywhere without my books; those are the most expensive things I own in life."

I took them from him and placed them neatly in my carry-on. They were the books Carol had recommended to me during my therapy sessions, the ones that had guided me through some of my darkest times. They weren't just books; they were a part of my journey and reminders of how far I had come. I packed each one carefully, remembering the hours I had spent reading them, underlining passages, and finding pieces of myself in their pages. These books had been my silent companions and were coming with me to Dubai through my transformation. I felt a wave of emotion when I stood back to look at the bags.

This wasn't just packing; it was the prize of everything I had worked for and fought for. And now, it was real. And in the blink of an eye, it was time to go to the airport. Walid couldn't come with me because he had to work, so we said goodbye at the house. As we stood by the doorway, the emotions hit us hard. He hugged me tightly, and before I knew it, we were both crying. He pulled back briefly, his face washed with tears, and said, "I didn't make it. I got the rejection email, but I didn't want to tell you and upset you."

My heart sank. I had been so consumed with my journey that I hadn't even thought about the possibility that Walid wouldn't make it. "Walid, I'm so sorry; you deserved it as much as I did."

He said, smiling through his tears. "No, this wasn't my dream. I went to the interview to support you and to give you emotional security. That's all. The biggest happiness for me is that you made it. This isn't about me. It's about you. This is your moment, not mine."

I hugged him again, holding him tightly as if to absorb some of his selflessness, love, and pride in me. Walid had always been my rock, my partner in this crazy journey, and now he was letting me fly, even though he wasn't coming with me.

"You're the best brother anyone could ask for. Thank you for everything."

"It feels like yesterday when we laughed at you for not knowing what a CV was. Look at you now, ready to roam around the world like a free bird. You'll do amazing; now go. Go live your dream. And don't forget to call me from Dubai, and if you meet a guy who breaks your heart, just call me, and I will break his face."

He made me laugh and cry at the same time with his comment. My heart was full of gratitude and sadness all at once. Leaving Walid behind was harder than I thought, but I knew he was right. This was my moment, my dream, and he had done everything he could to ensure I got here. As I climbed into the car, I looked back at him one last time, standing in the doorway with a bittersweet smile on his face. He gave me a little wave, and I waved back, knowing I would always carry his love and support with me no matter where life took me. As we drove to the airport, my mom kept smiling knowingly, as if she were hiding something. Finally, she looked at me and said, "There's a little surprise waiting for you at the airport."

I gave her a curious look. "What kind of surprise?" I asked, but she just shook her head, refusing to say more. I didn't press her, but the curiosity was killing me softly until we arrived at the terminal. When we arrived, I stepped out of the car, took a deep breath, and helped Baba with the bags. But then, as I turned around, I saw something that stopped me in my tracks. In front of me was a crowd of people, familiar faces, all smiling and waving, holding signs and teddy bears.

I blinked, my eyes widening in disbelief. It wasn't just my parents; Hamza and everyone else were there. All the girls from the office, Jill my hair-dresser, Chris my makeup girl, and my therapist, Carol, and all the people who had played a role in my journey, who had supported me through my struggles and helped me achieve my dream, were there, gathered at the airport to see me for one last hug before I was off to fulfill my destiny as a flight attendant. Tears filled my eyes as I stood there, overwhelmed by their love. They were holding little signs, waving, and calling my name.

"Nesrin!" they cheered. "We're so proud of you!" I couldn't help but laugh through my tears. It was such a surreal and beautiful moment. I ran toward them, hugging each of them, feeling gratitude for everything they had done for me.

"You didn't think we'd let you leave without saying goodbye?" Jill said, pulling me into a tight hug. "We are here to make sure that you don't change your mind about living in ugly Dubai," joked Chris with her unique sense of humor.

Even my colleagues from the office, the ones who had taught me so much, were there. "We're going to miss you," one of them said. "But we know you're going to shine and give us free Dubai tickets to visit you." And, of course, the other girls joining Dubai Airways with me were there, standing nearby with their families. They watched the scene unfold with wide eyes, probably wondering how I had managed to bring an entire crowd of supporters with me.

One whispered, "Wow, she brought half the city!" I overheard it and couldn't help but laugh; it was awkward and heartwarming. I hugged everyone tightly, tears flowing freely, as we all stood in that airport, tangled in emotions. There was so much love, so much pride, and so much sadness in that moment. Everyone had been a part of my story, and now it was time to close this chapter and step into a new one. I hugged my dad, crying, and I asked him for forgiveness for everything I have done, for every hard time I have given him, for disrespecting him multiple times and going against his will, for hurting him, and for many times making him feel small in front of our family members.

While hugging me back, he said that he had forgiven me, was proud of me, and would always be there, no matter what path I decide to take in life. When I said goodbye to Hamza, we cried like babies. It was a hard goodbye, and of course, he had to tell me to arrange a rich wife for him once I reached Dubai. When I hugged my mom, she apologized for everything, for not supporting me completely since the beginning; she said she felt she was harsh just like her father was with her, but it was to protect me and never to hurt me, and that I was becoming everything she ever dreamed of becoming, and that she was proud of me.

Then, just as I was trying to catch my breath, my mom touched my arm gently and said, "There's one more person who has to say goodbye to you."

I turned around, and there he was. Ziad. Standing just a few steps be-hind me, his expression was a mixture of sadness and pride. His presence hit me like a wave, and my heart broke when I saw him. I had deep feelings for him; leaving him behind felt like leaving a piece of myself. But I knew I had to. He walked up to me slowly, his eyes never leaving mine. "It's time, huh? "Yes, I can't believe it's actually happening."

He smiled faintly, a bittersweet look in his eyes, and said, "No matter where life takes us," he said, "I'll always remember you. And I'll always be supporting you, even if it's from far away. I'll always be clapping for you."

His words were always sweet toward me. At that moment, I felt a mix of love and sadness. Then he reached into his bag and pulled out a gift, a safe shaped like an ice cream cone. It was made of glass, colorful, and instantly familiar. "I brought you this. It's for you to save money. You can put coins in it piece by piece. And I made it an ice cream shape because... well, you know."

I smiled through my tears. The ice cream shop had always been our place, our sanctuary, where so many conversations had occurred. The safe wasn't just a gift; it was a memory, a piece of him I could carry wherever I went. I hugged him so tightly as if trying to make up for all the moments we would miss. For a moment, I didn't want to let go of him. I wish to take him with me and have his love and my dream. But that would be so selfish of me. He had other plans in life. He was building his career as a lawyer, opening his law firm in São Paulo; he had ambitions and dreams that were completely different from mine.

"Thank you, Ziad. Thank you for everything. For believing in me. For not giving up on me, and for me, everything was real too." His eyes filled with tears. After I said what happened between us wasn't just pretend, it wasn't just a fake marriage; it felt real, and I would have married him in another life. He held me for a moment longer before stepping back, looking into my eyes with a seriousness that took my breath away. "The moment you cross those gates, you won't be the same person ever again; even if you come back, you won't be the same."

I nodded, tears streaming down my face. "That's what I want, and I want the world to change me for the better. I want the experience, the growth, the pain, and the happiness. Everything I can get from the universe, I want."

With that, I turned to face the gate, my bags in hand, my heart heavier than ever. I waved my final goodbyes to everyone, my family, friends, and Ziad. They stood there, watching me take those last steps toward a life I had dreamed of for so long. As I reached the gate, I heard Ziad's voice call out one last time. "Nesrin!" I stopped, turning to look at him. His voice was steady, but his words carried so much weight.

"Today is April 24th. Happy Independence Day." I stood there and smiled, the significance of his words sinking in. This wasn't just my departure; it was my liberation, my freedom, my moment to become everything I had ever dreamed of being. Walking toward the restricted area, I whispered, "Happy Independence Day, Nesrin!"

I joined the other girls heading to Dubai, my heart still pounding with the mixed emotions I had left behind at the airport. As we boarded the plane,

I took a deep breath, realizing that this wasn't just a flight but the start of a new life. The hours on the plane felt endless, but they were filled with a strange energy, anticipation, hope, and a touch of fear. I kept looking out the window, imagining what awaited me in this city I had dreamed of for so long. When the plane finally began its descent, I felt my chest tighten.

After 15 hours, I was in Dubai. As I stepped off the plane, the warm air of Dubai hit me, carrying with it the promise of new beginnings. I moved through the airport with the other girls, equally nervous and excited. We went through immigration, cleared all the formalities, and it was time to enter the world. When I exited, I saw a familiar face standing among the crowd. It was Thalia.

She was waiting for me, her smile radiant and full of pride. When our eyes met, she opened her arms wide and said the words that made my heart swell, "Welcome home." I couldn't hold back. I dropped my bags and ran to her, wrapping my arms around her tightly. Tears streamed down my face, but they were tears of joy this time. Thalia had been my guiding light, the one who had always believed in me, told me that this day would come, and waited for me to come home.

And in that moment, I felt it. Dubai wasn't just a destination; it was the start of a new chapter, a new life, and a new version of myself. The girl who had fought for her dream, who had overcome rejection, heartbreak, and self-doubt, had finally arrived. As I stood there with Thalia, I knew this was where I was meant to be.

CHAPTER 21

Maktoub

القدر

And this is how my life as a flight attendant began. After all the suffering, the doubts, the rejection, and the heartbreak, I managed to wear that uniform, the one I had dreamed about for so long. The red lipstick. The red shoes. The scarf is around my neck. I was finally living the dream I had fought so hard to achieve. I traveled the whole world. I met incredible people from every nationality, every religion, and every walk of life. I tasted foods I'd never even heard of before. I lived independently, learned to care for myself, and even rescued street cats. I grew up in ways I never thought possible, learning responsibility, independence, and resilience. Of course, it wasn't always perfect. There were moments when I cried, moments when I laughed until my stomach hurt, and moments when I felt like giving up. I had my ups and downs, but every part of it, every single part, was worth it.

Dubai has always been my city of dreams, and it still is. I loved the chaos and unpredictability of being a flight attendant. I loved not knowing where I would be the next day; I loved the thrill of waking up in one country and falling asleep in another. I loved discovering new places, learning about different cultures, visiting temples, and exploring cities I didn't know how to pronounce. I embraced the crazy routine, the nights spent awake on flights, the jet lag, and the stolen snacks from minibars in hotel rooms. I loved the quiet moments in luxurious hotel beds, the wild nights out with friends I'd met along the way, and even the times when I cried alone in the middle of the night, feeling the weight of the journey. I loved every part of being a flight attendant and still love it. I still have a lot to discover, many people to meet, and many things to see.

Of course, not everyone was happy for me when I became a flight attendant. Success doesn't always bring cheers from the crowd. Many people, especially those from my village, tried to tear me down. They whispered behind my back, questioning my choices, saying that what I was doing wasn't respectable or appropriate for a girl from a conservative family. To them, I wasn't just a flight attendant; I was a girl who had broken off an engagement, left behind a traditional life, and chosen to travel the world alone. That was enough for them to judge, talk, and criticize me. My job didn't fit into the box they thought I should live in. They said things like, "What kind of girl does this?" or "She's brought shame to her family." But the truth was, I didn't care, and neither did my parents. For the first time in my life, I was living for me. Not for what people thought of me, not for the expectations placed on me by my culture or my village. I was finally free. I was feeding my soul with adventures, with life, with beauty. I filled my heart with memories from all over the world, learning and growing with every step I took. While they stayed in their same small circle, holding on to their narrow ideas of what a woman's life should look like, I was out there experiencing the world's infinite possibilities.

Yes, their words hurt sometimes. I would be lying if I said they didn't. But every time I stepped onto a plane, landed in a new country, and saw something breathtaking that made me realize how big the world truly is, their words faded into nothing. They didn't matter. What mattered was that I was happy. What mattered was that I was living my dream, building a life that was mine, and no one could take that away from me.

My parents didn't care about the gossip or the judgment. They knew what I had gone through to get here and were proud of me. That was all I needed. So, while they tried to eat me alive with their words, I chose to fly higher. Their opinions couldn't touch me anymore. I was too busy living a life that felt like freedom.

This life has pushed me to do things I never thought I was capable of. I've jumped from planes while skydiving, climbed mountains, walked across bridges and skyscrapers, and stood in awe of sights I never dreamed I would see. I've visited cities I didn't even know existed and found pieces of myself in every place I've been. I've learned so much, not just about the world but about myself. What else? What else? I've lived a life that so many people dream of living, and I am grateful every single day for the chance to keep living it. This life, the life I fought for, is mine, and it's everything I hoped it would be and more.

I spent hours discussing my whole story with my cousins Ikram and Youmna. It was already 5 am, and we were still awake. But my life story was so long, and they always wanted to know more and more, with full details. I told them that their parents, Aunt Rufaida and Uncle Mosab, were the members of the family who helped me the most and who always cheered for my happiness; even though it was early morning and the sun was about to rise, the girls still had questions. Youmna asked me with her eyes full of curiosity if I ever made it back to Brazil to see the people I had left behind after I became a flight attendant. I told her, "Yes," and it was very emotional.

When I arrived in Brazil, the first person I visited was Carol, my therapist. I wanted to thank her for everything she had done for me. She had been my anchor during my darkest moments, the person who believed in me when I couldn't believe in myself. As a token of gratitude, I brought her a doll, a little figure of a flight attendant dressed in the same uniform I wore daily. It looked like a miniature version of me. Carol hugged me tightly, and I could feel the pride she had for me. "You don't need to thank me; you did all the hard work, Nesrin. You're living proof that dreams come true."

Next, I went to see Jill, my hairdresser, the woman who had prayed for me and who had laughed and cried with me through the years. The one who used to wake up early to ensure I looked like the perfect flight attendant. She greeted me with her usual warmth, catching up as if no time had passed. I also took her a small souvenir, a miniature Burj Khalifa tower, so she could decorate her living room and remember that she made my dream come true. Then I asked about Chris; her face grew somber, and her eyes filled with water; as she looked down, she said, Chris isn't here anymore; she passed away a few months back. She had a heart attack."

Her words hit me like a punch in the chest. Chris, who always knew how to make me smile with her jokes, had prayed for me alongside Jill and Carol, was always ready with her makeup pouch, and woke up with the chickens early in the morning to support my dreams. She was gone. My heart broke as I asked for the address of where she was buried. I went to her grave alone. Standing by her stone, I felt an overwhelming sadness and an unbearable wish that she could be there to see the person I had become. I wanted to tell her everything: the places I had been, the people I had met, and my life. Tears poured down my face as I whispered, "Thank you for everything, Chris. I hope that your soul is at peace wherever you are."

All I had left of her now was the memory of her kindness and love. But I carried that memory as a part of my story and heart. I left by her gravestone the souvenir I had gotten her. It was a snowball with the Burj al-Arab inside.

When I got home, I noticed an envelope sitting on the table. My dad handed it to me without a word, and I opened it, curious. Inside was a beautifully designed invitation. My hands trembled slightly as I read the name Ziad.

It was his wedding invitation. He had found his soulmate, a Muslim girl, just like his parents always wished. Someone who matched the life he wanted and brought him happiness. I smiled, bittersweet. He deserved this happiness, and I was truly happy for him. My parents decided not to attend the wedding, but on the day of the ceremony, I couldn't help myself. I had to see him one last time. I didn't go inside or speak to him. Instead, I stood at a distance, watching him carry his bride into their new life together. He looked so happy, so content, and it filled my heart with peace to know that he had found the love and life he had been searching for. I didn't want to ruin his moment or disrupt his happiness, so I stayed in the background, unseen. I smiled through my tears, feeling grateful for the time we had shared, but knowing that chapter of our lives was closed now. As I walked away, I whispered under my breath, "Be happy, Ziad. You deserve it."

That trip to Brazil was a mix of emotions. I got to reconnect with people who had shaped my journey, but I also had to say goodbye to things I had once held close. It was a reminder that life moves forward and that some chapters close even as new ones begin. Before I returned to Dubai, I left on top of my mom's bed the gifts I had bought for her with a letter saying, "I was too young to understand your struggles and everything you sacrificed, everything you gave up, to raise us, to educate us, and to feed us. I know that life and people were not always kind to us. I know how much you have suffered and how much you have fought to give us a better life. Accept this gift as a thank you for everything you have done for me and my brothers, for being a strong mother who never abandoned her children even when the whole world was collapsing on top of you. Now, I can see and feel everything I didn't when I was just a child. Thank you for everything. I would like you to know that I would choose you as a mother in this life, in the afterlife, and in all lives over and over again. I love you."

I placed the letter on the bed, along with a jewelry box filled with some pieces of gold I had bought from Dubai. I remember all the times she would take us to another village to sell her gold to educate us, and I wanted to return it to her. Returning to Dubai afterward, I felt a new sense of purpose. The memories of the people I had seen, the ones I had loved and lost, stayed with me. They were a part of me, the main characters of my story. As I continued my life as a flight attendant, I carried those memories in my heart, knowing they had helped me become the person I am today.

"And this is the story of my life. My flight attendant life was happy, epic, messy, painful, crazy, and beautiful."

I said to Ikram and Youmna with a tear falling from the side of my eye, a tear of gratitude, and I continued, "Now it's time to go to sleep before Aunt Rufaida wakes up to pray and sees that we are all awake, and I'm going to take the blame for keeping you girls awake until late."

"Before we sleep, I just want you to know that you will always be my inspiration. I hope I have the same strength you have when I grow up, to fight for the things I want and dream about." Said Ikram.

"Ikram, this runs in the family. We come from a family with strong women who don't let anyone dictate our plans." I kissed both of my cousins goodnight and put them to sleep. I'm sure I overwhelmed them with my whole life story. It was too much to take in, but it was the truth, and they deserved to know it.

My divorce wasn't easy. Coming from a village where marriage is sacred and divorce is seen as a failure, I knew what I was walking into. The whispers, stares, and judgments came swiftly and without mercy. Facing the entire village as a divorced woman felt like standing in the middle of a storm, bracing myself against the wind. People didn't hold back. They said my marriage didn't work because it was my fault. Because I was a flight attendant. They believed I should fit in because I had dared to live outside the box. "She wasn't marriage material," they said. "She traveled too much. She was too independent. She should've stayed home." Hearing those words hurt deeply. It wasn't just the divorce that broke my heart; it was the relentless blame. They didn't know the truth of my marriage, of why it didn't work, but they didn't care.

They only saw what they wanted to see, and I became the easy target for their judgment. But I stood strong. I had been through too much in life to let this break me. I had fought for my dreams against all odds. I had faced rejection, heartbreak, and failure before, and I had risen every time. This was no different. I reminded myself that their opinions didn't define me. Their judgments didn't tell my story. I knew my truth. I knew the strength it took to leave a marriage that wasn't right for me, and I refused to let their words shake the foundation I had built within myself.

It took Samir two long years to divorce me. Two years of fighting in court, battling for my rights, not just as a woman, but as a human being who deserved freedom. As a Muslim, he had the right to move on, to remarry if he wished, even while we were still married. But I didn't have that right. I was trapped, unable to fully move forward with my life. And he knew it. He dragged it out on purpose, wanting to hurt me, to control me, even from far away. One day, I received a message from him: "I'll divorce you if you book me a ticket from Canada to Lebanon. Both ways."

He knew that, as his wife, I had travel benefits for him, and he intended to exploit them one last time. I knew he was using me, but I was desperate to end the chapter, to free myself from him. So, I did it. I issued him a round-trip ticket from Canada to Lebanon. He arrived in Lebanon, and finally, after two years of dragging me through pain, humiliation, and frustration, he divorced me. The courtroom echoed with finality as the proceedings concluded. I was free. But, of course, he should have known better. The world had changed me. I wasn't the same woman he had tried to control. As soon as the divorce was finalized and he left the courtroom, I canceled his ticket back to Canada. I imagined his face when he got to the airport, expecting to board his flight, only to realize the booking was gone. He had to buy his own way back. I didn't care. My battle was over, and I had won.

The first thing I did as a free woman was remember words my cousin Ikram said to me: "Yo, you can go to Paris, and he can go to hell." So, I booked a trip to Paris to celebrate my freedom. Standing in front of the Eiffel Tower, holding a box of colorful macarons, I felt a joy I hadn't felt in years. I wore a vibrant, flowery dress, a cute little hat perched on my head, and my favorite pair of heels. I sat by the edge of the iconic Parisian landscape, savoring each macaron like it was a victory because it was. As I looked at the Eiffel Tower, I felt a wave of gratitude for how far I had come. This wasn't just about being free from Samir; it was about being free from the constraints of other people's judgment and living the life I had fought so hard to build. As I sat there, a message appeared on my phone. It was from a girl in my village. She wrote, "I've been following your story. Becoming a flight attendant has become my dream, too. Can you help me?"

I stared at the message, stunned. For years, my village criticized and judged me for choosing this path. They said I wasn't respectable, that I wasn't worthy, that I had brought shame to my family. And now, this girl was inspired by me, asking for my guidance. At that moment, I realized I wasn't a source of shame but a beacon of hope. My story had become a symbol for the younger generation, proof that it was possible to fight for your dreams and win. I wasn't just living for myself anymore. I paved the way for others to claim their freedom, live their own truth, and chase their dreams.

So, I answered her with a text back, with my heart full of hope that I could start changing the mindset of people in that village and bring the new generation to freedom. I replied, "Let's chase that dream and build your wings."

About Nasso Haymour

Nasso Haymour is a woman who refused to be caged by expectations. Born into a world where tradition dictated a woman's role, she defied the odds to pursue her dream of becoming a flight attendant—a path that challenged deep-rooted cultural norms and tested her resilience at every turn.

From a young age, Nasso knew she was destined for more than what was expected of her. While others urged her to conform, she chose to break free, proving that ambition, perseverance, and self-belief can overcome even the strongest barriers. Her journey was far from easy—she faced criticism, societal judgment, and personal sacrifices—but she refused to surrender to a life dictated by others.

Through her memoir, *Breaking the Cage*, Nasso shares her deeply personal story of love, defiance, and freedom, offering a voice to countless women who have ever been told their dreams were impossible. With unfiltered honesty, she recounts the battles she fought, the lessons she learned, and the price of choosing independence over acceptance.

Her story is not just about breaking traditions—it's about redefining what it means to be a woman, to dream without limits, and to live life on one's own terms.

Having traveled the world, Nasso has carried with her not just stories of distant places, but the wisdom, strength, and courage that come from daring to be different. She continues to inspire women everywhere to chase their dreams—no matter the cost.